Dale Earnhardt Jr.

Other books in the People in the News series:

people in the NEWS

Dale Earnhardt Jr.

by Laurie Collier Hillstrom

LUCENT BOOKS
A part of Gale, Cengage Learning

GALE
CENGAGE Learning™

Detroit • New York • San Francisco • New Haven, Conn • Waterville, Maine • London

GALE
CENGAGE Learning

LIBRARY OF CONGRESS CATALOGING-IN-PUBLICATION DATA

Hillstrom, Laurie Collier, 1965-
  Dale Earnhardt, Jr. / by Laurie Collier Hillstrom
    p. cm. — (People in the news)
  Includes bibliographical references and index.
  ISBN 978-1-4205-0088-2 (hardcover)
  1. Earnhardt, Dale, Jr.—Juvenile literature.
  2. Automobile racing drivers—United States—Biography—Juvenile literature. I. Title.
  GV1032.E18H56 2009
  796.72092—dc22
  [B]
                                                                    2008029081

Lucent Books
27500 Drake Rd
Farmington Hills MI 48331

ISBN-13: 978-1-4205-0088-2
ISBN-10: 1-4205-0088-0

Printed in the United States of America
1 2 3 4 5 6 7 12 11 10 09 08

Contents

Fame and celebrity are alluring. People are drawn to those who walk in fame's spotlight, whether they are known for great accomplishments or for notorious deeds. The lives of the famous pique public interest and attract attention, perhaps because their experiences seem in some ways so different from, yet in other ways so similar to, our own.

Newspapers, magazines, and television regularly capitalize on this fascination with celebrity by running profiles of famous people. For example, television programs such as *Entertainment Tonight* devote all their programming to stories about entertainment and entertainers. Magazines such as *People* fill their pages with stories of the private lives of famous people. Even newspapers, newsmagazines, and television news frequently delve into the lives of well-known personalities. Despite the number of articles and programs, few provide more than a superficial glimpse at their subjects.

Lucent's People in the News series offers young readers a deeper look into the lives of today's newsmakers, the influences that have shaped them, and the impact they have had in their fields of endeavor and on other people's lives. The subjects of the series hail from many disciplines and walks of life. They include authors, musicians, athletes, political leaders, entertainers, entrepreneurs, and others who have made a mark on modern life and who, in many cases, will continue to do so for years to come.

These biographies are more than factual chronicles. Each book emphasizes the contributions, accomplishments, or deeds that have brought fame or notoriety to the individual and shows how that person has influenced modern life. Authors portray their subjects in a realistic, unsentimental light. For example, Bill Gates – the cofounder and chief executive officer of the software giant Microsoft – has been instrumental in making personal computers the most vital tool of the modern age. Few dispute his business savvy, his perseverance, or his technical expertise, yet critics say he is ruthless in his dealings with competitors and driven more by his desire to maintain Microsoft's dominance in the computer industry than by an interest in furthering technology.

In these books, young readers will encounter inspiring stories about real people who achieved success despite enormous obstacles. Oprah Winfrey – the most powerful, most watched, and wealthiest woman on television today – spent the first six years of her life in the care of her grandparents while her unwed mother sought work and a better life elsewhere. Her adolescence was colored by promiscuity, pregnancy at age fourteen, rape, and sexual abuse.

Each author documents and supports his or her work with an array of primary and secondary source quotations taken from diaries, letters, speeches, and interviews. All quotes are footnoted to show readers exactly how and where biographers derive their information and provide guidance for further research. The quotations enliven the text by giving readers eyewitness views of the life and accomplishments of each person covered in the People in the News series.

In addition, each book in the series includes photographs, annotated bibliographies, timelines, and comprehensive indexes. For both the casual reader and the student researcher, the People in the News series offers insight into the lives of today's newsmakers – people who shape the way we live, work, and play in the modern age.

Living Up to the Family Name

Since the founding of NASCAR (National Association for Stock Car Auto Racing) in 1948, a number of families have made important contributions to the sport of stock-car racing. Many of the men who became involved in the sport during its early years shared their passion for racing with their sons, helping to build future generations of drivers, race team owners, and pit crew members. Of all the families that contributed to the development, growth, and exploding popularity of NASCAR racing, however, one name stands above all the others: Earnhardt.

The patriarch of the family, Ralph Earnhardt, was the most dominant driver in the sport during the 1950s and 1960s. His son, Dale Earnhardt Sr., won seven Winston Cup championships between 1980 and 1994, tying the great Richard Petty for the most titles in NASCAR history. In many ways, the tough, aggressive style of Dale Sr.—known as The Intimidator and The Man in Black—became the image of NASCAR during his reign. Both of the elder Earnhardts were inducted into the International Motorsports Hall of Fame in Talladega, Alabama, and featured on a 1998 list of NASCAR's 50 Greatest Drivers.

As the son and grandson of these NASCAR legends, Dale Earnhardt Jr. faced high expectations when he first started driving race cars in 1992. Many people assumed that his famous name and family connections gave him an easy path into the world of racing. In reality, though, Junior had to work his way up through the ranks like any other young driver. He received very little help

Two generations of racing's legendary Earnhardt family, Dale Jr. in the number 8 car and Dale Sr. in the number 3 car, take to the track in Daytona Beach, Florida in 2001. Today, Junior continues the tradition of racing excellence that began with his grandfather Ralph in the 1950s.

or support from his father during his early racing career. As had been the case throughout Junior's childhood, Dale Sr. was simply too busy with his own career to spend much time with his son. So Junior charted his own course into auto racing. He built and repaired his own cars, gained experience and confidence, and gradually moved up through NASCAR's racing divisions.

Only after Junior proved that he had the skill and determination to be a successful driver did his father hire him to represent his race team, Dale Earnhardt Inc. (DEI), in the Busch Grand National Series (called the NASCAR Nationwide Series starting in 2008). Junior responded by winning two consecutive Busch Series titles in 1998 and 1999. His success earned him a promotion to the Winston Cup Series (called the Sprint Cup Series starting in 2008)—the big leagues of NASCAR racing—in 2000. Junior made an impressive debut, winning two races and nearly earning rookie of the year honors during his first full season on the circuit.

Like his father and grandfather before him, Junior loved being a professional race-car driver. "There's nothing better and nothing I'd rather do than be going around the track in a race car," he stated. "That's something I've fallen in love with and don't want to give up for a long time."[1] But he also found that joining the Winston Cup circuit brought him another important benefit: It allowed him to develop a closer relationship with his father. Even though they competed against each other during the 2000 season, Dale Sr. and Junior spent quality time together at the track and established a deeper level of love, respect, and understanding than they had ever achieved before.

Tragically, this father-son bond was shattered during the first race of the 2001 season. Dale Earnhardt Sr. was killed in an accident on the final lap of the Daytona 500. The loss of stock-car racing's most prominent personality stunned NASCAR drivers and fans, but it hit Junior hardest of all. As he struggled to overcome his grief, he also had to deal with the enormous pressure that settled upon him as the heir to the Earnhardt legacy.

Following the death of his father, Junior became the main focus of attention for millions of NASCAR fans. He inherited many of Dale Sr.'s followers, but he also earned many of his own. In 2003 Junior was voted NASCAR's most popular driver for the first time. The following season he cemented his place as the sport's biggest star by claiming an emotional victory in the Daytona 500, three years after his father had lost his life in the same race.

Although Junior experienced ups and downs on the track over the next few seasons—finishing well in some races but also having accidents and mechanical failures—he remained NASCAR's most popular driver. In addition, his good looks, laid-back attitude, straight-talking charm, and regular-guy sensibility gave him a unique, crossover appeal that attracted legions of new fans to stock-car racing. Junior accounted for 30 to 40 percent of NASCAR's $2 billion in annual merchandise sales, and a poll conducted by MSNBC.com ranked him as the fifth-most-marketable athlete in the United States.[2]

Even as his popularity skyrocketed, however, Junior felt growing dissatisfaction with his roller-coaster racing career. He longed to perform consistently through an entire season and compete for a championship. "I just like running up front [among the race leaders] every week," he explained. "I want to be up front and challenging, and when I show up at the track I want people to expect me to run well."[3] Over time, Junior became convinced that DEI—which had come under the control of his stepmother, Teresa Earnhardt, following his father's death—was not willing or able to commit the resources required to help him reach his goals.

In 2007 Junior sent shock waves through the world of NASCAR by announcing that he would leave his family's race team at the end of the season. He then signed a contract to drive for Hendrick Motorsports—the most successful and technologically advanced team in the sport—beginning in 2008. Junior hoped that this change in direction would ultimately help him live up to the family name. "I understand that I have no more excuses. Now I'll have the best equipment and the best people behind me. It's time for me to start winning," he declared. "I do know that my daddy would be damn envious of me right now."[4]

Chapter 1

Son of a Racing Family

Ralph Dale Earnhardt Jr.—known in racing circles as Junior— was born on October 10, 1974, in Kannapolis, North Carolina. Located about 30 miles (48km) north of Charlotte, Kannapolis was the home of many NASCAR drivers, crew members, and race shops. In fact, it was sometimes called "Car Town" because many of the streets were named after car models and engine parts. Junior's father, Ralph Dale Earnhardt Sr. (known as Dale), was a young race-car driver who was just beginning to make a name for himself. Junior's mother, Brenda Gee Earnhardt, was Dale Sr.'s second wife.

Junior's family tree is large and complicated. His father was married three times and had four children. Junior has an older half brother, Kerry, from his father's first marriage. Kerry lived with his mother, Latame Brown, so the two boys did not get to know each other until their teen years. Junior also has a sister, Kelley, who is two years older. Since they have the same mother and father, they grew up together and are very close. Junior's parents divorced in 1978, when he was four years old. A few years later, Dale Sr. married Teresa Houston. They eventually had a daughter, Taylor.

Many members of Junior's family were involved in auto racing. His grandfather, Ralph Lee Earnhardt, was one of the top drivers in the early years of NASCAR. He won more than five hundred races in his career and was champion of the National Sportsman Series (which later became the Busch Grand National Series) in

Ralph Lee Earnhardt, Junior's grandfather, was a top driver in the early days of NASCAR.

1956. Junior's other grandfather, Robert Gee, was a well-known race-car builder. In addition, several of Junior's uncles and cousins worked in race shops or as members of pit crews.

Grows Up Around Racing

This family background ensured that racing was always a part of Junior's life. As a boy, he enjoyed hanging around the busy, noisy garage where his father's race team built and fixed cars. He liked to watch the mechanics work and listen to the drivers talk. Junior also loved to attend his father's races. He did not get this opportunity very often, so it always felt like a special treat. "Everything in life was all about getting to the race track," he

The Earnhardt family—from left, Dale Sr., stepmother Teresa, sister Kelley, and Junior—gathers in New York in December 1998.

remembered. "But you didn't go unless you were asked. So the night before you'd hang out with [Dad] while he watched television, just hoping he might say something. Everything was about getting next to a race car."[5]

Outside of the garage and the track, Junior did not spend much time with his father. From the age of four, when his parents divorced, until he was eight, Junior and his sister Kelley lived with their mother. In 1982, after Dale Sr. remarried, they moved into their father's house in Mooresville, North Carolina. By this time, Dale Sr. had already won his first Winston Cup championship. The successful driver traveled all over the country to compete in races, drive test sessions, and make public appearances. He also invested in several North Carolina Chevrolet dealerships. This busy schedule meant that he was rarely at home with his family. "When I started driving, I put everything else in second place," Dale Sr. acknowledged. "There were tough times and I missed so much of my kids' growing up."[6]

A Brief History of NASCAR

After World War II ended in 1945, a thriving auto-racing culture developed in the American South. All across the region, young men got together on weekends to race souped-up cars on country roads and oval dirt tracks. These events were not well organized and used many different sets of rules.

Bill France Jr. was a mechanic, driver, and promoter in the auto-racing scene in Daytona Beach, Florida. Frustrated with the lack of organization at these racing events, France arranged a big meeting with interested drivers, race promoters, and track officials. They decided that they could improve the quality of auto racing by establishing a sanctioning body for the sport. They founded the National Association for Stock Car Auto Racing (NASCAR) on February 21, 1948. This new organization brought order to the sport and ensured that various racing leagues used a common set of rules for tracks, cars, and drivers.

NASCAR held its first race in the "strictly stock" class—which later became the Sprint Cup Series—at Charlotte Speedway (now Lowe's Motor Speedway) in North Carolina on June 19, 1949. Over the next half century, the sport exploded in popularity. By 2008 NASCAR sanctioned about fifteen hundred events at a hundred tracks across the country each year. The most famous NASCAR race series is the Sprint Cup (formerly known as the Winston Cup and as the Nextel Cup, the name changes when the sponsor changes), followed by the Nationwide Series (formerly known as the Busch Grand National Series and Late Model Sportsman Series).

Despite Dale Sr.'s frequent absences, Junior admired his father greatly. He was impressed by the older man's hard-driving style and tough, intimidating image. In fact, Junior thought Dale Sr. was so cool that he had trouble imagining himself ever following in his father's footsteps. "When I was a little kid, I played with

Stock cars compete on the shore of Daytona Beach, Florida, in February 1955 in an early NASCAR event.

Matchbox cars and I always made myself a winner. I raced against Daddy's competitors, but there was a small thought in my mind that racing was never going to be a reality for me," he acknowledged. "I'm 4'10" as a freshman in high school. How am I going to become some kick-ass race car driver?"[7] Instead, Junior usually pictured himself becoming a mechanic for a race team.

Despite his self-doubt, Junior loved cars and had racing in his blood. When his family went to the go-kart track, he was a surprisingly aggressive driver. The karts were not equipped with seat belts, and he admitted that he "came flying out of them quite often."[8] Dale Sr. remembered watching Junior compete in a go-kart race when he was about ten years old. After starting in the middle of the pack, Junior charged up on the outside and tried to pass the second-place kart. "Dale Junior's wheel got clipped and he went up into the air, tumbling head over heels," his father recalled. "About the time he had stopped I had run across the track and was standing there, and he said, 'Where's my go-kart?' The only thing he was concerned about was 'Where's my go-kart?' That was a pretty awesome sight, I'll tell you."[9]

Although Dale Sr. appreciated his son's competitive spirit, he still did not expect Junior to take up auto racing. "I never thought Dale Jr. was going to be a driver," he stated. "He never seemed to have the interest. He wasn't one of those kids who always wanted to be around the garage, to see how things worked."[10] Since Junior was shy and suffered from low self-esteem, he had trouble communicating his interest in the sport to his father.

Focuses on School

Whatever career path Junior chose, Dale Sr. felt strongly that his son needed a good education to be successful. "I always wanted Dale Jr. to get an education," he noted. "I always talked about that. My biggest regret is that I dropped out of school in ninth grade. My father told me it was a mistake. I just wouldn't listen. I wanted to make sure Dale Jr. didn't make the same mistake."[11]

In order to keep his son's focus on school, Dale Sr. made Junior follow strict rules. "I was kind of sheltered," Junior remembered. "My daddy didn't let me go out much. I couldn't go out with my buddies to the mall. I couldn't skip school. My dad wouldn't put up with that crap."[12]

When Junior entered his teens, he had trouble getting along with his stepmother, Teresa. Dale Sr. was not usually around to help enforce the rules, so they decided to send Junior away to military school for his middle-school years. Since Junior was small for his age and very quiet, his sister Kelley worried that he might become a target for bullies. She knew that being the child of a famous race-car driver could also create problems for him at school. "The thing about NASCAR fans is they either love you or hate you," she explained. "The ones who love you, they love you all the way. They know everything about your life, everything about your family's lives. There aren't any secrets. The fans who hate you, well, they can't stand anything about you. It can be a

Dale Earnhardt Sr.

NASCAR legend Dale Earnhart Sr.—known as The Intimidator and The Man in Black—was born on April 29, 1951, in Kannapolis, North Carolina. As the son of a well-known race-car driver, Dale Sr. developed a love for cars and racing at an early age. He dropped out of school at age sixteen to work as a mechanic and pursue his dream of driving race cars.

After working his way up through various levels of competition, Dale Sr. appeared in his first Winston Cup race in 1975. He made his debut as a full-time Winston Cup driver in 1979. After a strong performance that included a race victory and a seventh-place finish in the season point standings, he was named Rookie of the Year. In 1980—only his second full year on the circuit—Dale Sr. claimed the Winston Cup Championship.

Dale Sr. soon became the most dominant driver in Winston Cup racing, winning six more titles between 1986 and 1994. His total of seven championships tied with Richard Petty for the most in NASCAR history. Dale Sr. also won seventy-six career races and earned $41 million in prize money. He capped his career by winning the Daytona 500 in 1997, on his twentieth attempt.

Throughout his racing career, Dale Sr. was known as an aggressive and determined driver who would do almost anything to reach the checkered flag first. His hard-driving style, as well as his reputation as an unpretentious Southern good old boy, made him the most popular personality in the sport. Dale Sr.'s millions of fans went into mourning on February 18, 2001, when he was killed in an accident on the final lap of the Daytona 500. His famous number 3 still appears on countless caps, shirts, flags, and window stickers across the nation.

problem either way. Being two years older than Dale Jr., I guess I took on the role of protective sister."[13]

Junior eventually returned home and attended the public schools. He graduated from Mooresville High School in 1992.

NASCAR legend Dale Earnhardt Sr., known as the Intimidator because of his hard-charging style on the track, dominated Winston Cup racing in the late 1980s and early 1990s, earning seven titles and millions of loyal fans.

Considering the strong emphasis his father placed on education, Junior was deeply disappointed when Dale Sr. did not show up for the ceremony. "Education. Yeah, it was such a big thing," he related. "So I graduated from high school, and where was my father? He didn't come to graduation. He was in a race somewhere. I understand now, of course, but I was looking forward to holding that diploma in his face. Except he wasn't there."[14]

Junior went on to earn an associate's degree in automotives from Mitchell Community College in Statesville, North Carolina. Since the college was known locally as Mitchell-In-Town, Junior often joked that he had attended MIT (the prestigious Massachusetts Institute of Technology, usually called MIT). After graduating, he took a job as a mechanic at one of his father's Chevrolet dealerships. He liked to boast that he became the fastest oil-change man in the shop within a matter of weeks.

Builds His Own Stock Car

In the meantime, Junior was also taking his first steps into the world of stock-car racing. During Junior's senior year of high school, he and his half brother, Kerry, had decided that they wanted to try auto racing. They got very little support from Dale Sr., who was determined not to give his sons any special treatment. By this time, the elder Earnhardt had won four NASCAR Winston Cup titles and ranked among the most popular drivers in the country. He also owned a successful race team, Dale Earnhardt Inc. (DEI). Nevertheless, Dale Sr. felt it was important for his sons to work their way up in the sport, the way his own father had made him do.

Junior was not too excited about the idea of starting at the bottom of his father's racing enterprise. "I always wanted to be a driver," he noted. "There was always this idea, though, that you had to sweep the floor for a year before you ever got a chance to touch a wrench. I didn't want to sweep the floor."[15] Instead, he and his brother decided to launch their own racing effort. They bought a 1978 Chevrolet Monte Carlo at a junkyard and began fixing it up. The only help they received from their father came

Junior received little support from his father at the start of his racing career, so learning the family business on his own in early races such as this Legends Series event (Junior is in the outside lane) increased his independence and skill.

in the area of safety equipment. "I put in a good set of roll bars, a harness, straightened out all the safety stuff. Then I let them do the rest themselves," Dale Sr. remembered. "Safety was my one concern."[16]

After fixing up the car, Junior and Kerry took turns driving it in short-track races in NASCAR's Street Stock division. Their father never attended the races and offered Junior very little encouragement or advice. "Dale made him use his own money and get his own sponsors just like he had to do," recalled Junior's uncle and DEI crew chief, Tony Eury Sr. "Dale wouldn't give it to him."[17] The lack of fatherly support bothered Junior at times, but it also made him more independent and self-confident. As the months passed by, Junior showed growing signs that he had the skill, determination, and desire to become a successful driver.

Chapter 2

Making His Own Mark

After graduating from high school in 1992, Junior continued racing in NASCAR's Street Stock division. He also attended the Fast Track driving school at Charlotte Speedway (now Lowe's Motor Speedway). Junior impressed the instructor, NASCAR veteran Andy Hillenburg, with his aggressive driving style and determination to improve his skills.

Before long, other influential people started to take notice of Junior's talent. Former NASCAR driver Gary Hargett—a longtime friend of Dale Sr.—saw the young man race in the Street Stock division at Concord Motorsport Park. Hargett informed Dale Sr. that his son had a great deal of potential. He offered to let Junior race one of his old cars in the Late Model Stock Car division (an entry-level NASCAR series in which older cars compete in local or regional races) if Dale Sr. agreed to pay for a new engine and tires.

Dale Sr. resisted his friend's idea at first. He still felt it was important for Junior to make his own way as a driver. Over time, though, the elder Earnhardt grew impressed with his son's effort. Since Junior had demonstrated a willingness to work hard, Dale Sr. rewarded him by helping him move up into Hargett's car.

Gains Valuable Racing Experience

Racing in the Late Model Stock division turned out to be a great learning experience for Junior. He polished his driving skills on

Stock Cars

One of the main rules of NASCAR is that the racing machines have to be "stock" cars. This means that the cars must be based on the models sold in automobile dealerships. In the early days of NASCAR, the cars that competed in races were nearly identical to those that rolled off factory assembly lines. To be considered stock cars, vehicles could only be modified to include better safety equipment. Over time, as stock car racing expanded in size and popularity, NASCAR allowed further modifications to increase the level of competition.

The cars used in the NASCAR Sprint Cup Series today are still based on four-door, American-made models, including the Ford Fusion, Dodge Charger, Chevrolet Monte Carlo, and Toyota Camry. But the vehicles that race around high-banked oval tracks at speeds of over 200 miles per hour (322kmph) barely resemble those that people drive on the nation's highways. Instead, they have evolved into high-performance racing machines with big engines, wide tires, and aerodynamic bodywork. The race versions weigh 3,400 pounds (1,542kg), have 110-inch (279cm) wheelbases, and feature 358-cubic-inch V8 engines (5,867cc) that generate over 750 horsepower.

Even though today's stock cars are true racing machines, they are still sturdier than the custom-built, open-wheeled sports cars used in Formula One and Indy Car racing. The fact that NASCAR racers have full bodywork rather than open wheels, for instance, allows the drivers to engage in more crowd-pleasing rubbing and bumping on the track.

short tracks throughout the South. He faced fierce competition from other young drivers who were hoping to prove themselves and move up to higher levels of racing. Some of these drivers were resentful of Junior. They thought that he was there because of his famous name. They sometimes made a point of bumping his car to show that they did not plan to give him special treatment. But these experiences helped further Junior's development.

The cars used in NASCAR races have evolved from vehicles with specifications nearly identical to those driven by average Americans in the 1940s and 1950s into high-performance machines with custom engines, tires, and body designs.

Instead of shying away from this hostility, he learned to channel his anger and frustration and set aside distractions.

Junior raced in the Late Model Stock division for three full seasons, from 1994 to 1996. His results were solid, but not spectacular. In 113 races, he qualified on the pole (posted the fastest qualifying time to earn the right to start the race in first place) twelve times and earned three victories. He also showed great consistency by earning ninety top-ten finishes. Junior enjoyed everything about this early racing experience. "I helped put together, work on, and set up my cars. I learned from my mistakes," he recalled. "I wasn't a dominating driver, didn't win many races, but I was consistent."[18]

Joins the Busch Grand National Series

Junior's performance in the Late Model Stock division earned him an opportunity to showcase his talents in the Busch Grand National Series. The Busch Series (now called the Nationwide Series) was widely considered to be the top training ground for young stock-car

Junior competes in a Busch Series race in Homestead, Florida, in November 1997, the last of eight Busch events he entered that year. He achieved his first Busch Series victory in April 1998.

racers. Like the minor leagues in professional baseball, it gave drivers a place to showcase their skills and prepare for the big leagues of NASCAR racing—the Winston Cup (now called the Sprint Cup) Series. A Busch race usually took place on a Saturday at the same track where the Winston Cup race was held on Sunday.

Junior recognized that appearing in the Busch Series marked a big step up in his racing career. "I was having fun driving late-model cars. Just messing around," he acknowledged. "When I started running Busch, I got serious. Everything about that was cool."[19] Junior was not just aiming to impress race-team owners and sponsors, though. He was also hoping that a strong performance in the Busch Series would bring him closer to his father. "Sure, I was seeking my father's approval," he admitted. "I wanted to make him proud. I'd been trying to do that all my life."[20]

Junior made his first start in a Busch race in Myrtle Beach, South Carolina, in 1996. He qualified seventh and finished a respectable fourteenth in that event. In 1997 he appeared in eight Busch Series races and earned one top-ten finish. As the start of the 1998 NASCAR season approached, Dale Earnhardt Inc. (DEI) needed to hire a new driver for the Busch Series. Junior's uncle and DEI's crew chief, Tony Eury Sr. tried to convince Dale Sr. to keep the job in the family. He argued that if Dale Sr. was going to invest in a young driver anyway, his son had shown as much promise and ambition as anyone else.

Week after week, the opening remained unfilled, even though Junior drove the DEI car in preseason tests. Finally, just before the season started, Junior learned that he would be representing the DEI team full time in the Busch Series. "[My father] avoided talking to me about it. I didn't know for sure that I was the driver until the name decals came into the shop two weeks before Daytona," he remembered. "I know he just wants to teach me respect. He didn't want me to assume."[21]

Celebrates First Busch Series Victory

Junior made his mark early in the 1998 Busch season. He claimed his first victory on April 4 at Texas Motor Speedway in Fort Worth,

Texas. Racing the number 8 that had once adorned the car of his grandfather, Junior started in the middle of the pack and gradually worked his way up toward the front. By the time a caution flag came out with eleven laps to go in the race, he was third behind Glenn Allen and Joe Nemechek. Allen spun out a few laps later, but Junior stayed out of trouble. He passed Nemechek for the lead on the last lap and held on for the win.

After the race ended, an excited Dale Sr. rushed to his son in Victory Lane (the area where the winners go to celebrate after the race) and gave him a big hug. "That was pretty awesome, wasn't it?" the veteran driver gushed. "I couldn't be prouder. That felt as good as it did when I won the Daytona 500."[22] Junior later described his dad's reaction as one of the most emotional moments of his life. "It stirred memories of the years I had tried so hard to earn my dad's approval," he stated. "Maybe that did it. It really was a proud moment for him to show that much excitement and happiness over something that I had accomplished."[23]

Earns Back-to-Back Busch Series Titles

The emotional victory in Texas was just the beginning of a remarkable 1998 season for Junior. He went on to win six more races that year and claim the Busch Series championship. Junior thus followed in the footsteps of his father and grandfather before him and became the first third-generation driver to win the Busch title.

At the end of the 1998 season, Junior signed a six-year sponsorship deal with Budweiser worth an estimated $40 million. He emphasized that his family connections had nothing to do with it. Instead, he claimed that he earned it with his performance on the track. "I definitely had to work my way up the ranks," he noted. "I would hope that people would look at my accomplishments and realize that I have had to make a name for myself."[24]

The 1999 season started out slowly for the defending Busch Series champion. Mechanical problems and accidents led to disappointing finishes for Junior at several early races. At midseason,

Junior celebrates his second Busch Grand National Series championship in November 1999.

however, he recovered and roared to victories in three races in a row. He finished the season with six wins, which vaulted him to a second consecutive series championship. Junior thus joined Sam Ard (1983–1984), Larry Pearson (1986–1987), and Randy LaJoie (1996–1997) as one of the four drivers ever to win back-to-back Busch Series titles.

Wins over Fans

By the time Junior claimed his second championship, he had become the most popular driver in the Busch Series. He received more requests for interviews—and was followed by more fans seeking autographs—than any other driver. He undoubtedly got some extra attention because of his famous name. But many people also appreciated his hip clothing, laid-back personality, and hard-charging driving style.

Junior was often in the middle of the action in Busch races, and he enjoyed giving fans something interesting to watch. He described his racing style as "aggressive, more so at times than it should be, relative to the way NASCAR runs the series. I enjoy that kind of racing, hate watching a race that looks like a bunch of toy soldiers marching around. Fans like action, even if their favorite driver gets bumped around or spun out."[25]

Having a Famous Name

In his best-selling book *Driver #8*, Dale Earnhardt Jr. describes his feelings about belonging to a racing family:

I'm a member of my own generation, but I never forget I am also the son of a racing legend and grandson of another famous racer, Ralph Earnhardt. Being the son and the grandson of these two tough guys definitely hasn't hurt my career. And you will *never* hear me complain about being brought up with the name Dale Earnhardt Jr. But don't for one minute believe that I had everything handed to me, though. If you knew my father, you would never think that.

Dale Earnhardt Jr. with Jade Gurss, *Driver #8*. New York: Warner Books, 2002, p. 32.

Many fans also supported Junior because of his steady improvement. His early experiences building and fixing his own race cars gave him a strong understanding of mechanical issues. He thus developed the valuable ability to troubleshoot problems and recommend changes to his pit crew in midrace. "He's got a good feel for the car. He's not scared of it. He's not afraid to make changes," said fellow driver Bobby Labonte. "If they do make a change, he can go out and feel it and say, 'This is what the car is doing.' And they always make it better. Then you throw all that out the window, and he's a great driver on top of that."[26]

Races Against His Father

Junior's success in the Busch Series gave him the opportunity to appear in five Winston Cup races during the 1999 season. He was thrilled to race in the big leagues of NASCAR, especially because it meant that he would share the track with his father. "I just wanted to be out there on the same straightaway, to watch him right in front of me,"[27] Junior admitted. He was disappointed when his father did not seem to share his excitement about the occasion. "He approached it just like it was any other race,"[28] he recalled.

The two Earnhardts faced each other in a Winston Cup race for the first time on May 30, 1999, at Lowe's Motor Speedway outside Charlotte, North Carolina. Junior started an impressive eighth out of forty-three cars. He was unhappy with the way his car handled throughout the race, however, and was unable to run with the leaders. Still, Junior stayed out of trouble and finished a respectable sixteenth, ten positions behind his father. "It was a lot of fun," he said afterward. "I hope those drivers out there are a little bit more comfortable with me. I was just trying not to tear up a race car and earn some respect, and to learn something from running around with them out there."[29]

A more exciting father-son matchup took place a few weeks later, at an International Race of Champions (IROC) event at Michigan International Speedway (MIS). The IROC series con-

Junior and Dale Sr. pose with their cars and racing teams before the NASCAR Thunder Special Motegi Coca-Cola 500 in Motegi, Japan, in November 1998, the first race in which the Earnhardts competed against each other. The following May, they shared the track at a Winston Cup event for the first time at Lowe's Motor Speedway near Charlotte, North Carolina.

sisted of four one-hundred-mile races (161km) between twelve identical cars, driven by the top drivers from various racing series, including NASCAR, IndyCar, and Formula One. The idea was to create a test of pure driving skills that would determine the ultimate champion from different types of racing. Junior was invited to participate as the 1998 Busch Series champion, and his father earned a spot by finishing among the Winston Cup leaders. They both jumped at the chance to compete in the IROC series.

The race at MIS turned into a battle between the two Earnhardts. On the last lap, Junior was running second behind his father. He tried to pass on the outside of the final turn, but the wily veteran had other ideas. Junior remembered:

It came down to the last lap between my father and me—Big E and Little E side by side, banging fenders all the way across the finish line… I had him beat, but his fishing buddy, Rusty Wallace, came up at the end and gave him a big push. They're big rivals when there's Winston Cup points on the line, but that day they were like ol' buddies. It was a photo finish and they wound up calling my father the winner by a coat of paint. When we goof around, we still argue about it. It was one of the most exciting and fun races we ever ran in.[30]

Chapter 3

Death of a Legend

Afterwinning two consecutive Busch Series championships, Dale Earnhardt Jr. moved up to race full time in the Winston Cup Series in 2000. The Winston Cup (now called the Sprint Cup) Series is the highest level of NASCAR racing. The drivers race for higher stakes, represent bigger sponsors, receive more publicity, attract more fans, and face greater pressure than those in other NASCAR series.

The biggest Winston Cup race of the year is the Daytona 500. It is also the first race of the season, held in February in Florida. Drivers and teams begin preparing for the famous race almost immediately after the previous season ends. Junior had appeared in five Winston Cup races during the 1999 season, but he still felt a thrill at the thought of competing in his first Daytona 500. "The history and the prestige of this place are just so immense that I can't wait to say I've raced in the Daytona 500," he recalls in his book, *Driver #8*. "I'm usually pretty calm once I'm inside the car, but today I'm unbelievably anxious."[31]

Driving the red number 8 Chevrolet sponsored by Budweiser and owned by his father's team, Dale Earnhardt Inc. (DEI), Junior qualified eighth overall. After starting the race on the outside of the fourth row, he found it difficult to be patient. As the race unfolded, Junior took advantage of every opportunity to improve his position, but he did not show much interest in cooperating with his DEI teammates. He ended up finishing thirteenth, which was considered very respectable for a rookie, and he beat his father for the first time in Winston Cup competition. But Dale Sr., who finished twenty-first, was not pleased with the way his son conducted himself on the track. "Junior didn't work at all with anybody," he told reporters afterward. "He wanted to pass. That's all he wanted to do, so that's why he finished where he did."[32]

Wins His First Winston Cup Race

Junior learned from his mistakes and performed well in the next few races. On April 2, 2000, the Winston Cup Series went to Texas Motor Speedway in Fort Worth, Texas, for the DirecTV 500. This track was one of Junior's favorites. Two years earlier, it had been the site of his first victory in the Busch Series. He was pleased with his car throughout the practice and qualifying sessions, and he felt very confident when the race began.

After starting in the fourth position, Junior roared to the front of the pack and ran among the leaders all day. He built up a huge lead in the final few laps. "The car is unbelievable," he says in *Driver #8*. "The red Bud machine streaks away from the rest of the field. I am able to stretch the margin to more than six seconds (an eternity in NASCAR racing)."[33] Junior thus claimed his first victory in only his twelfth career Winston Cup race (it had taken his father sixteen races to reach his first Winston Cup win).

When Junior arrived in Victory Lane, his father—who had finished seventh—rushed to greet him. "I never saw [Dale Sr.] as proud in his life as he was the day Junior won his first Winston Cup race," recalled friend and fellow driver Jimmy Spencer. "I felt so happy for them that day."[34]

Junior was thrilled to finally earn the respect of his father and other Winston Cup veterans. "It was fun to get out front and show these guys I could use my head and make smart decisions," he noted. "Even when I've got a real fast car and I'm not up front, I can be patient and I can pick my way up through there. It was fun to prove that to them and prove my status as far as drivers go."[35]

Becomes a Rookie Sensation

A month later Junior proved that his victory in Texas was no fluke when he won the Pontiac Excitement 400 in Richmond, Virginia. This time, though, the finish was much closer. Junior

Confetti flies as Junior celebrates being the first rookie driver to win the Winston All-Star Exhibition Race at Lowe's Motor Speedway near Charlotte, North Carolina, in May 2000.

beat NASCAR veteran Terry Labonte to the finish line by 0.159 seconds. The razor-thin margin of victory gave Junior two wins in his rookie season. "We are the first team to take two races this season," he wrote. "Rookie team. Rookie driver. Winners, not just once, but twice."[36]

Junior's hot streak continued the following week, when he became the first rookie driver ever to win the Winston All-Star Exhibition Race at Lowe's Motor Speedway in North Carolina. Afterward, he gave the credit to his crew for preparing an outstanding car. "When the car is this good, it's hard to describe the feeling of power and strength," he explained. "The team and I joke about it, but it's like you're invincible and you just need to tell the other guys to get the hell outta our way or be crushed by our superior strength."[37]

The superiority of the Budweiser number 8 car became clear to fans toward the end of the race. Junior found himself in tenth place after a pit stop with just eight laps to go. But he blasted through the field like a rocket, passing his father for second place, and then speeding past veteran driver Dale Jarrett for first. "I couldn't believe it," Dale Sr. said afterward. "I thought I could get up there to give Jarrett some trouble and I looked in the mirror and here this red thing comes!"[38]

Grows Closer to His Father

For Junior, one of the best things about his rookie Winston Cup season was that it brought him closer to his father. The two men spent time together at the track and talked to each other more often than before. They enjoyed sharing stories and joking around during interviews and photo shoots. They both found that competing against each other had actually strengthened their relationship. "I'm going through a lot of the things my father's been through, and I'm starting to understand him more," Junior acknowledged. "We're able to relate to each other easier."[39]

Some longtime Winston Cup competitors noticed a change in Dale Sr.'s attitude and performance once his son joined the circuit. "When Dale Jr. began racing in Winston Cup, it totally

Junior and Dale Sr. appear before a race at Michigan Speedway in Brooklyn, Michigan, in August 2000. Race observers found that the Earnhardts' time together at the track as competitors on the Winston Cup circuit that year allowed them to create new bonds in their relationship as father and son.

changed Dale Sr.'s outlook on things," said fellow driver Dave Marcis. "He became more competitive and rejuvenated."[40] The elder Earnhardt's new dedication to racing brought him to the brink of a record eighth career championship. In the end, though, he had to settle for a second-place finish in the 2000 Winston Cup point standings.

In the meantime, Junior was the top candidate for the Raybestos Rookie of the Year Award for much of the Winston Cup season. This honor is presented each year to the first-year driver who earns the most points in his best seventeen finishes. Unfortunately for Junior, his luck ran out toward the end of the 2000 season. A series of accidents and mechanical problems caused him to drop in the point standings, enabling Matt Kenseth to claim the award.

Junior still made an impressive debut, finishing sixteenth in the Winston Cup point standings. Many observers predicted that the young driver would contend for the championship once he gained more experience and maturity. Junior admitted that these factors had contributed to his problems during the second half

"I Know a Man . . ."

During his rookie Winston Cup season, Dale Earnhardt Jr. wrote an occasional column for NASCAR Online. A few months before Dale Earnhardt Sr.'s death, Junior contributed a moving tribute to his father titled "I Know a Man. . . ." It read in part:

> This man could lead the world's finest army. He has wisdom that knows no bounds. No fire could burn his character, no stone could break it. . . .
>
> I have had the pleasure of joining him on the battlefield. I have experienced his intimidating wrath. . . . He roams like a lion, king of his jungle. His jungle is his and his alone. Every step he takes has purpose. Every walk has reason.
>
> He praises God, loves his family, enjoys his friends.
>
> I wonder what his future holds. He has so much to be proud of. To this point, he's only barely satisfied. His eyes see much more than my imagination could produce. He is Dale Earnhardt.
>
> Dad, the world's finest army awaits.

Dale Earnhardt Jr., "I Know a Man. . . ." NASCAR Online. Reprinted in Dale Earnhardt, Jr., with Jade Gurss, *Driver #8*. New York: Warner Books, 2002, p. 263.

of his rookie season. "The majority of the time, my crew and I were on the same page," he noted. "Then there were times when we weren't even reading the same book or speaking the same language. It's mainly due to a lack of communication."[41]

Junior's success on the Winston Cup circuit in 2000 greatly expanded his fan base. He won over many of his father's followers and also earned some of his own. Encouraged by the strong fan interest, Junior wrote a book about his rookie season called *Driver #8*. It provides a race-by-race account of his experiences, as well as some insights into his relationship with his father. The book proved to be extremely popular with NASCAR fans and spent more than three months on the *New York Times* best-seller list.

Tragedy Strikes

The Earnhardt family anticipated the start of the 2001 Winston Cup season with excitement. Junior was determined to use everything he learned to improve upon his rookie performance. Dale Sr. hoped to build upon his successful 2000 season and become the first driver ever to win eight career Winston Cup titles.

As always, the first race of the season was the Daytona 500. Following two tension-filled weeks of practice sessions and qualifying races, the big event finally took place on February 18, 2001. The DEI team—which included Junior, his father, and Michael Waltrip—ran extremely well all day. As the race entered its final few laps, the DEI cars held the top three positions. After leading for seventeen laps, Dale Sr. fell back to third place behind Waltrip and Junior with one lap remaining. Hoping to ensure victory for a member of his race team, the veteran driver did his best to prevent other cars from passing him and challenging for the lead.

As the field reached the final turn, fellow driver Sterling Marlin bumped into Dale Sr. The NASCAR legend lost control of his black number 3 Chevrolet and crashed into the concrete retaining wall on the outside of turn four at 180 miles per hour (290kmph). He bounced back onto the track, where he was hit by Ken Schrader, then hit the wall again and careened across the track onto the infield grass. Just as the

Junior crosses the finish line at the 2001 Daytona 500 while smoke from Dale Sr.'s crash at Turn 4 of the final lap rises from the track behind him.

accident occurred, Waltrip crossed the finish line for his first Winston Cup victory in 463 tries. Junior finished close behind in second place.

At first, few people among the drivers, spectators, and television viewers watching the race suspected that Dale Sr.'s accident was serious. During his long racing career, he had survived many wrecks that looked worse. Shortly after the race, however, drivers and fans alike were stunned to hear that the crash had taken the life of Dale Earnhardt Sr. He had died instantly from severe head and neck injuries.

Struggles with Grief

When news of Dale Sr.'s death became public, all of NASCAR mourned the loss of a legend. The Intimidator had defined the

Junior pauses at a news conference at North Carolina Speedway near Rockingham, North Carolina, during a discussion about his father, who was killed only a week earlier at the Daytona 500. Although he chose to compete at the Rockingham event, he crashed his car in the first lap.

NASCAR Safety Equipment

The death of Dale Earnhardt Sr. highlighted the dangers of auto racing and led to a reexamination of the sport's safety practices. NASCAR requires race cars to be equipped with a variety of safety gear to help drivers survive crashes at speeds of over 180 miles per hour (290kmph).

One of the most important safety features on stock cars is the roll cage. Made of strong metal tubing, it acts like a skeleton underneath the external bodywork. The windshields of NASCAR racers are made of a heavy-duty shatterproof plastic called Lexan that absorbs impact. The roofs have special flaps that reduce lift and prevent the cars from becoming airborne in a crash.

The interior of NASCAR racers also has a number of safety features. A specially molded seat holds the driver securely around the hips, ribs, and shoulders. The driver also wears a restraint system made of nylon straps that are much wider and stronger than the seatbelts in a passenger car. The straps form a five-point harness that goes over both shoulders, across the lap, and between the legs. Side window nets made of nylon webbing help to keep the driver's arms inside the vehicle if it rolls over.

NASCAR drivers wear special racing suits made of fire-retardant materials. In addition to the racing suit, the driver's uniform includes gloves, socks, shoes, and a hood called a balaclava. The drivers also wear padded helmets with hard shells to protect their heads. Since the death of Earnhardt Sr., NASCAR has required drivers to use a head and neck support (HANS) device. This device is intended to prevent whiplash-type injuries that occur when the driver's head is left unsecured while his body is strapped into the seat.

sport of stock-car racing and inspired undying loyalty and admiration in millions of race fans. In the midst of a huge national outpouring of grief, however, no one took Dale Sr.'s death harder than his son. "I lost the greatest man I ever knew, my dad," Junior

Junior dons his helmet and HANS device, two of the many pieces of equipment that protect NASCAR drivers from injury in the event of a crash.

remembered. "There were no guidebooks, no rules, no script about how to act or how to grieve. The first three or four days after the crash were the emptiest days of my life. I don't know how I remained strong. I had such a weight on my chest. But my family was there for me, and I was there for them."[42]

A few days after the accident, thousands of people gathered to honor Dale Earnhardt Sr. at a memorial service at Cavalry Church in Charlotte, North Carolina. Junior struggled to deal with his feelings of grief. He missed his father every moment and wondered how he would be able to continue without him. "As I walked out of the memorial service for Dad on a bitterly cold, dreary, rainy day, I felt like I was walking into my future. I was now on my own," he recalled. "But I knew he had raised me to be my own person and that somehow I would find the strength and the guts to carry on."[43]

Junior ultimately decided that the best way to honor his father was to become the best driver—and the best person—that he could possibly be. He vowed to be more mature and take racing more seriously. "The secret to all the success I've had is my dad. It's that simple. He taught me how to drive, how to live with integrity, and how to be a man,"[44] he noted. "[Losing someone like that] shows you how conceited you are, how trifling you can be, how selfish you are. It's really changed me 100 percent, hopefully into a better person."[45]

Makes a Comeback

Not surprisingly, it took some time for Junior to truly overcome his loss. Although he joined the field for a race at Rockingham, North Carolina, the week after his father's death, Junior seemed distracted. He crashed his car on the very first lap and finished last. He did poorly in the next few races on the Winston Cup schedule, as well. "Junior is obviously going through a tough time right now," said his friend and fellow driver Matt Kenseth. "But he'll get through this. He'll persevere. He's a tough guy."[46]

Junior's performance improved gradually, and he posted several top-ten finishes as the 2001 season went on. On July 7, the series returned to Daytona for the Pepsi 400. It was the first Winston Cup race to be held at the track since his father's death, and the first one in more than twenty years not to feature Dale Sr. among the competitors.

In the weeks leading up to the race, Junior dreaded the idea of returning to Daytona. He worried that his emotions would overwhelm him. Once he arrived at the track, however, he felt his father's presence all around him. He found that it helped him to relax and feel comfortable. "I had everything that he had, knowledge and confidence," Junior recalled. "I just felt like I couldn't be touched."[47]

The Pepsi 400 turned out to be one of the best races of Junior's career. He dominated the field, leading 116 out of 160 laps. Although he was forced back to seventh place by a multiple-car accident with six laps remaining, he quickly fought his way back to the front. Junior's victory was assured when his DEI teammate Michael Waltrip—who had won the Daytona 500 on the day that Dale Sr. was killed—passed veteran Bobby Labonte on the last

Junior leads the celebration of his victory at the Pepsi 400 at Daytona International Speedway in July 2001, a win he dedicated to his late father.

lap to move into second place. Waltrip prevented any competitors from catching Junior, and the DEI drivers captured the top two positions at Daytona for the second straight race. This time, however, Junior crossed the finish line first.

Junior became emotional in Victory Lane as he dedicated his first win of the season to his father. "Man, I just don't know what to say," he stated. "He was with me tonight. I don't know how I did it. I dedicate this win to him."[48] Many fellow drivers and countless NASCAR fans were pleased for Junior. They felt that the race results were appropriate for the occasion and would have made Dale Sr. proud.

Junior continued to race well for the remainder of 2001. He claimed another emotional victory at Dover International Speedway in Delaware in the first Winston Cup race to be held after the September 11 terrorist attacks. He won a third time at Talladega Superspeedway in Alabama, which had been the site of his father's final career victory a year earlier. Junior's three wins and fifteen top-ten finishes helped him end the season ranked eighth in the Winston Cup point standings. It was a solid performance for any second-year driver—but especially for one who had to overcome the tragic loss of his father at the start of the season.

Chapter 4

Triumph at Daytona

Following the death of his famous father in the 2001 Daytona 500, Dale Earnhardt Jr. realized that the time had come for him to grow up and be his own man. The tragedy forced the promising young driver to become more independent and work to establish his own identity, both on and off the track. "After my dad's death I struggled to figure out who I was,"[49] he acknowledged.

At the same time, though, Earnhardt emphasized his desire to continue his father's legacy. "I don't feel like I've got to get out from under my dad's shadow," he stated. "He was awesome. If I'm half as good as he was or accomplish half as much as he did, I'll be really happy with my career. The biggest compliment you can pay me is that I remind you of my dad."[50]

Earnhardt first demonstrated his newfound maturity by accepting a larger role in the management of his father's business interests and race team. At the start of the 2002 season, he became co-owner of Chance 2 Motorsports with his stepmother, Teresa. Dale Sr. had started the race team nearly a decade earlier. By 2002 it had grown into a successful Busch Series team, built around Martin Truex Jr., a promising young driver. Truex went on to win back-to-back Busch Series championships in 2004 and 2005, just as Earnhardt had done early in his racing career. Earnhardt also launched a new race team in 2002 called JR Motorsports. It started out by sponsoring cars in the Late Model Sportsman division at Concord Motor Speedway, where Junior had been introduced to the sport.

The NASCAR Point System

As of 2008, the NASCAR Sprint Cup season consists of thirty-six races held on twenty-two different tracks across the country. All but two of these races take place on high-banked oval tracks. Although these tracks vary in length from 2.5-mile (4km) superspeedways to 0.5-mile (0.8km) short tracks, all of the races go counterclockwise and the drivers make only left-hand turns. Two annual Sprint Cup races take place on twisting road courses—at Watkins Glen in New York and Sears Point in California—where the drivers must shift gears, brake, and turn both directions.

All thirty-six Sprint Cup races are worth the same number of points in the season standings (the only exceptions are the Budweiser Shootout and the Sprint All-Star Exhibition Race, which are special events that do not award points). For each race, drivers receive points based on their finish positions. The winning driver is awarded 185 points, for instance, while the second-place driver receives 170 and the third-place driver earns 165. From there, the number of points awarded drops gradually for each finish position. The last-place driver receives thirty-four points for finishing forty-third in a race.

Sprint Cup competitors can also earn up to ten bonus points in each race. Any driver who leads a lap receives five bonus points. In addition, the driver who leads the most laps in a race is awarded five bonus points. The NASCAR scoring system is designed to reward drivers for performing consistently through the entire season. Only drivers who rank among the top twelve in total points—regardless of how many races they have won—are eligible to compete for the season championship.

Earns Respect

After his father's death, Earnhardt also showed greater maturity on the track. During the 2002 Winston Cup season, he continued to learn, improve his skills, and earn the respect of his fellow drivers. The season started badly for Earnhardt, though. In April he crashed during a race at California Speedway and suffered a

Earnhardt holds the trophy awarded to him for his third-place finish in the 2003 Winston Cup point standings.

concussion. Although he did not admit to the head injury for several months, it affected his performance on the track. In fact, Earnhardt failed to place higher than thirtieth in his next three races. But he came back later in the season to win both Winston Cup races at Talladega Superspeedway and post six top-ten finishes in the last eight races of the year. These late-season results helped lift him to a respectable eleventh place in the point standings.

Earnhardt worked hard during the off season in an effort to make a bigger splash in 2003. He approached his career with greater focus, discipline, and preparation than ever before. Earnhardt started a fitness program, showed up on time for test sessions and public appearances, and reorganized his pit crew. His efforts paid off in a breakout season that placed him in contention for the Winston Cup championship.

Unlike the ups and downs of previous seasons, Earnhardt's performance was very consistent throughout 2003. He finished in the top five in an impressive thirteen events. He won at Talladega in April—making him the first driver ever to win four consecutive races at the fabled superspeedway—and chalked up another victory at Phoenix International Raceway in Arizona in November. Unfortunately for Earnhardt, his friend and rival Matt Kenseth had an even better year and ran away with the Winston Cup title. Earnhardt finished a career-high third in the point standings, though, and also won the National Motorsports Press Association's Most Popular Driver Award for the first time.

Makes a Statement at Daytona

As Earnhardt and the other drivers prepared for the 2004 season, NASCAR made several important changes to its premier racing series. First, the Winston Cup became the Nextel Cup after NASCAR decided to change its primary sponsor to Nextel Communications. Although the Winston cigarette brand had been involved with stock-car racing for more than thirty years, NASCAR severed its ties to tobacco in hopes of expanding its appeal to young people. In order to add excitement to the Nextel Cup season, NASCAR also introduced a ten-race playoff system called the Chase for the Cup.

These changes had little impact on the Daytona 500, which remained the traditional opening race of the 2004 season. It also

Earnhardt's crew rushes to greet him as he leaps from his car following his victory at the Daytona 500 in February 2004.

maintained its status as the most popular NASCAR event among fans, and the most prestigious race for drivers to win. Although Daytona held special meaning for many people, it was particularly important to Earnhardt. He always felt close to his father when he competed at the fabled track, and he longed to win the big race in his father's honor. "All of the things that have happened in the past have made us work harder to try to win this race," he admitted. "I'm not ashamed to say I put a lot of emphasis on coming down here and winning this race because of what I have been through down here."[51]

After weeks of anticipation, the Daytona 500 finally took place on February 15, 2004. From the time the green flag dropped, it was clear that Earnhardt was the driver to beat. He led the first twenty-nine laps and never fell out of contention all day. The race eventually came down to a duel between Earnhardt and Tony Stewart. On lap 181 out of 200, Earnhardt made a daring move to take the lead. Just when it looked as if he was going to attempt to pass Stewart on the outside, he dove to the inside and streaked past his opponent. Stewart stayed close until the end, but he could not find a way to get by Earnhardt's superior machine.

After the race ended, some people suggested that Stewart had let Earnhardt win the race out of respect for his father. Stewart

The Chase for the Cup

In 2004—the year Dale Earnhardt Jr. won the Daytona 500— NASCAR made a major change to its traditional system of awarding driver points. It introduced a playoff system called the Chase for the Cup. Under this system, only the top twelve drivers in the point standings at the end of twenty-six races are eligible to compete for the annual series championship.

Junior's longtime friend and rival Matt Kenseth was mostly responsible for NASCAR instituting this change. During the 2003 season, Kenseth accumulated such a huge lead in the point standings that he locked up the title with several races remaining. With much of the drama removed from the end of the season, NASCAR experienced a significant decline in ticket sales and television ratings.

NASCAR devised the Chase for the Cup to add excitement and increase the likelihood that the championship would not be decided until the last race of the season. At the end of twenty-six races, each of the twelve Chase qualifiers has his season point total reset to five thousand, plus ten additional points for every race he won during the season. This system effectively wipes out any big lead in points that a driver may have accumulated through the first three-quarters of the season. During the ten-race Chase, points are awarded in the same way as the regular season. The driver who has the most points at the end of the season wins the championship.

Drivers who do not qualify for the Chase continue to compete based on the points they accumulated throughout the season. To encourage competition, the top non-Chase driver—who automatically finishes thirteenth overall in the standings—receives a million-dollar prize.

insisted that the idea was ridiculous. "I'd love to have won the race, trust me," he declared. "I did everything I could to still win the race. If I could have held him off, had him finish second, I would have done it in a heartbeat. But there was no holding that kid back today. Today was his day."[52]

Earnhardt was thrilled to claim one of the biggest prizes in auto racing in only his fourth attempt. His victory came six years after his father won the only Daytona 500 of his legendary career, and three years after his father lost his life in the race. "This is like you can't write a better script,"[53] he said afterward. "Some of our greatest competitors come in and out of this sport without taking this trophy home. I'm glad I can say I accomplished it and I can put the ongoing striving to win it behind me. It's just the greatest race. It's the greatest day of my life. I can't really describe it. I don't know if I will ever be able to tell this story to anybody and really get it right."[54]

Gets a Scare

Winning the Daytona 500 was a great start to the 2004 season for Earnhardt. He hoped to build upon that early success throughout the year and earn a spot in the inaugural Chase for the Nextel Cup. In July, however, Earnhardt was involved in a fiery crash that almost cost him his life.

During a weekend off from NASCAR racing, Earnhardt decided to test his skills by racing a Chevrolet Corvette in an American LeMans Series event in Sonoma, California. On the first lap of a practice session, Earnhardt's car spun off the track backward and hit a concrete barrier. The impact ruptured a fuel line, causing the car to burst into flames. Earnhardt struggled to unbuckle his safety harness and climb out of the cockpit. "The heat got up to more than 1,000 degrees," he remembered. "I was in the car for 14 seconds. I do feel that my dad was with me. I heard someone holler, 'Come on! Come on! Get out!' Yet nobody was there."[55]

Earnhardt's flame-retardant driver's suit offered some protection from the fire, and it may have even saved his life. But he still suffered second- and third-degree burns on his legs, neck, and chin. Earnhardt tried to compete in a Nextel Cup race the fol-

Crews tend to Earnhardt's burning car after a crash at an American LeMans Series race in Sonoma, California, in July 2004. Earnhardt suffered severe burns in the wreck.

lowing weekend, but he had to drop out due to pain and fatigue. Earnhardt not only had to heal his physical wounds, but he also had to recover his mental edge. The frightening incident forced him to face his own mortality for the first time. "I know when I go out there I could die," he stated. "But if I quit driving cars because of that, I wouldn't be living."[56]

Finishes Strong

Earnhardt proved that he had overcome his injuries—and his fears—in August by winning the Sharpie 500 at Bristol Motor Speedway in Tennessee. This famous short track is known for producing very tight races, as well as spectacular multiple-car wrecks. Earnhardt was pleased to claim the thirteenth victory of his career at Bristol, which had been the site of some of his father's greatest races. "This is huge for me; it's awesome for our team. We really needed that," he said afterward. "My dad made this place magic for Earnhardt fans, and I was one of them. He was The Man. Wherever he's at, he's laughing."[57]

Earnhardt hoists the winner's trophy after his victory at the EA Sports 500 at Talladega Superspeedway in Talladega, Alabama, in October 2004.

Following the win at Bristol, Earnhardt and his number 8 car went on a hot streak. He claimed yet another victory at Talladega Superspeedway in October by mounting a tremendous late charge. After leading much of the race, Earnhardt dropped back to eleventh place following a pit stop with five laps to go. He quickly made up the lost positions, however, with a series of expert moves. Earnhardt passed Kevin Harvick to regain the lead and never looked back. The impressive victory allowed him to move into first place in the 2004 Nextel Cup standings.

Unfortunately for Earnhardt, his reign as the series points leader did not last long. In his excitement over the victory, he used a swear word during a live television interview from Victory Lane. NASCAR officials imposed a twenty-five-point penalty on him for violating its rule against drivers using obscene language. Earnhardt fought the controversial penalty, which also carried a ten-thousand-dollar fine, but he lost his appeal. When the points were deducted from his season total, he dropped down to second place in the standings.

Despite the swearing incident, Earnhardt still ended up with plenty of points to qualify for the ten-race Chase for the Nextel Cup. He failed to finish two of the Chase races, however, and slipped to fifth place in the final season standings. Nevertheless, Earnhardt had one of the best years of his career in 2004. He won six races, including the Daytona 500. He also showed great consistency by finishing in the top five in sixteen different events. To top it off, Earnhardt collected a career-high $7.2 million in prize money and earned the Most Popular Driver Award for the second year in a row.

Chapter 5

The Face of NASCAR

Earnhardt's terrific 2004 season firmly established him as a NASCAR star in his own right. As he prepared to start his fifth full season on the circuit, fans and competitors alike viewed him with respect as a veteran driver. Earnhardt enjoyed his new status and eagerly accepted the responsibilities that came with it. "I turned 30 last year, and it was like, overnight, I got into a mentality that I'm going to make some decisions for myself," he stated. "I'm not going to worry about the things I used to worry about as much and take more control of things."[58]

As Earnhardt embraced his independence, he continued to develop an identity that was separate from that of his famous father. "Dale Jr. is doing a pretty good job of being his own man," said NASCAR legend Richard Petty. "He seems to know what he is and where he is, and he is doing the best he can as Dale Jr. There won't be another Dale Earnhardt, but there won't be another Dale Earnhardt, Jr., either."[59]

Earnhardt still carried enough of his father's legacy to remain popular among Dale Sr.'s fans. They appreciated his hardworking, down-to-earth image, as well as his love for auto racing and its history. Yet Earnhardt also attracted thousands of fans of his own—many of whom were new to NASCAR. This new generation of fans was drawn to his good looks, casual style, hip interests, and direct approach to dealing with the media.

The Popularity of NASCAR

NASCAR's popularity grew rapidly during the 1990s and early 2000s. During this period, stock-car racing expanded beyond its roots in the rural South to appeal to an estimated 75 million devoted fans across the country. Attendance at races increased over time to reach an average of more than 130,000 spectators per event. Millions more fans tuned in on television, helping to make NASCAR the second most-watched sport on American TV after professional football.

During this period, NASCAR fans became known for showing intense loyalty to their favorite drivers. They spent more than $1 billion each year on clothing and other merchandise bearing the name, car number, or image of their heroes. As NASCAR's popularity exploded, many high-profile corporate sponsors competed to place their logos on cars, drivers' suits, and team merchandise. Stock-car racing also entered mainstream popular culture through the release of successful films like *Cars* and *Talladega Nights: The Ballad of Ricky Bobby*.

After fifteen years of rapid growth, however, some analysts claimed that NASCAR's popularity leveled off in 2006. Only half of that season's races sold out, and TV ratings declined for many events as well. Some critics claimed that the thirty-six-race Sprint Cup season lasted too long to hold fans' attention. Others argued that the retirement of several popular veteran drivers contributed to a reduction in fan interest. NASCAR officials, though, blamed the decline on a general downturn in the U.S. economy and insisted that the sport remained vital and healthy.

Liz Clarke, "While NASCAR Takes Stock, Racing's Popularity Wanes," *Washington Post*, November 4, 2007.

Updates NASCAR's Image

Unlike many other popular drivers, Earnhardt's appeal extended well beyond the world of stock-car racing. He not only became the face of NASCAR, but he also emerged as the sport's first crossover star. In addition to being voted NASCAR's most popular

Fans pack the stands at the 2008 Daytona 500, the premier race for the NASCAR loyal. After becoming wildly popular in the 1990s and early 2000s, interest in NASCAR has leveled off in recent years.

driver in 2004, for instance, Earnhardt was named one of *People* magazine's fifty most beautiful people in the world. Another poll found him to be the fifth-most marketable athlete in the United States, behind only golfer Tiger Woods, basketball star LeBron James, and NFL quarterbacks Tom Brady and Peyton Manning.

Earnhardt's celebrity has grown beyond the NASCAR world, leading him to non-racing business opportunities such as the Whisky River Nightclub in Charlotte, North Carolina, which he opened in 2008.

Many observers felt that Earnhardt's popularity helped expand interest in NASCAR racing nationwide. "Junior's the right guy at the right time," said former driver and TV commentator Darrell Waltrip. "He's young. He's good looking. He's single. He likes to do the things a [young] guy likes to do. He connects with the MTV crowd and the computer geek. That's why our sport is so healthy right now. We're capturing a more mainstream audience early on."[60]

Earnhardt's widespread appeal brought him all kinds of opportunities that were not available to other NASCAR drivers. He was paid to endorse sophisticated products, such as Drakkar Noir cologne. He also got the chance to develop video games, appear in music videos, and star in a series of public-service announcements promoting the use of seat belts. Shortly before the start of the 2005 Nextel Cup season, Earnhardt was the subject of an in-depth interview with journalist Mike Wallace that aired nationally on the TV news program *60 Minutes*.

Earnhardt also launched his own media production company, called Hammerhead Entertainment. He produced and hosted several shows about auto racing, including *Shifting Gears* for the cable TV network ESPN2 and *Dale Earnhardt Jr.'s Unrestricted* for XM Satellite Radio's Sports Nation. Earnhardt also served as the host of a show called *Back in the Day* for the Speed television network. This program examined the roots of NASCAR, showed footage from early races, and traced some of the changes that have taken place in the sport over the years. Earnhardt's fame also led to small roles in two major Hollywood films about auto racing, the animated *Cars* and the live-action comedy *Talladega Nights: The Ballad of Ricky Bobby*.

In addition to opportunities in media and entertainment, Earnhardt's celebrity also created many business opportunities for him. He took advantage of this situation to open a bar in downtown Charlotte, North Carolina, called Whiskey River, introduce a candy bar called Big Mo', and help design and build a new racetrack, Alabama Motorsports Park near Mobile, Alabama. Some people claimed that Earnhardt's fame extended further than any driver in NASCAR history. "I don't know if I ever had that kind of popularity," said the sport's second-most-popular driver, Jeff

Gordon. "If he wins the championship . . . game over for anybody else. We [fellow drivers are] not even going to exist out there."[61]

The Downside of Fame

Although Earnhardt enjoyed many aspects of his growing celebrity, he disliked some other aspects. For instance, he faced constant demands on his time for interviews, public appearances, and promotional events for NASCAR and his sponsors. His busy schedule gave him a new perspective on the pressures that his father had faced during his career. "Now I understand some of

Earnhardt fans clamor for autographs before qualifying rounds for the Pocono 500 at Pocono Raceway in Long Pond, Pennsylvania, in June 2006.

what he was going through all those years," he stated. "There are a lot of people tugging at you all the time."[62]

At the racetrack, one of Earnhardt's biggest challenges was dealing with fans. Whenever he stepped out of his motor home—whether he was on his way to a drivers' meeting, a practice session, or an interview—he was immediately mobbed by fans asking for autographs. He did not mind signing a few items when he had time, but the sheer number of people made it impossible to satisfy everyone. Disappointed fans sometimes became angry and shouted at him or tried to block his path.

Junior's Sanctuary

Every successful NASCAR driver attracts a following among race fans. But Dale Earnhardt Jr. is far and away the most popular among the sport's stars. Since Earnhardt receives constant attention from adoring fans wherever he goes, he has turned his home into a private retreat where he can enjoy all of his favorite activities in the company of family and close friends.

Earnhardt lives on 140 acres (57ha) of land outside Mooresville, North Carolina. His house is modest, but his property features a swimming pool; a regulation boxing ring; a six-hole, par-three golf course; and an elaborate go-kart track with a vintage Union 76 gas station. Earnhardt's property even includes a custom-built replica of an Old West frontier town, complete with saloon, general store, church, hotel, and jail.

Earnhardt also enjoys hanging around his house and playing racing video games or tinkering around with computers. His home serves as a sanctuary from the pressures of his very public life. "When I'm here, nobody judges me. I get to be who I want to be and act like I want to act," he explained. "The worst part about this place is as soon as you leave, you're missing it. . . . I just like it. I feel real OK here."

Seth Livingstone, "Hanging Out with Junior," *USA Today*, January 12, 2007.

Earnhardt sometimes found that the constant attention from fans and reporters made it difficult for him to concentrate on his job. The intense spotlight also made him feel as if he had to be careful about everything he said or did. "Two years ago, when I'd walk from my motorcoach to the car in practice, there were less than half the people asking for autographs, so I see that there's a big change as far as the hard-core fans that we have now," he acknowledged. "There's a responsibility that goes with it now. A lot of the fans say, 'Man, we like you because you're yourself—stay yourself, always be yourself.' And that's true to a point, but I'm finding now, more and more, that we're under the microscope, that some of the things I would do in the past aren't accepted now."[63]

While Earnhardt felt a responsibility to be accessible to his fans, he became upset when people refused to respect his privacy. On many occasions, fans jumped over his security fence and wandered around his property, hoping to catch a glimpse of his home. "They'll just assume that it doesn't bother me if they walk through the woods to see it," he explained. "They're gonna assume, 'Junior don't care. He's a great guy. He's OK with everything.' That's really the reputation I've got."[64]

Rough Times on the Track

As Earnhardt's fame grew, some observers wondered how it would affect his racing performance. They questioned whether all the attention from fans—combined with his increasing involvement in a variety of outside business interests—would take a toll out on the track.

At times, these concerns seemed well founded. For example, Junior had several heated arguments with his crew chief, Tony Eury Jr. toward the end of the 2004 season. When news reports about these clashes leaked out, it became even tougher for the cousins to resolve their problems. "We took it out on each other,"[65] Eury Jr. acknowledged. The high-profile disputes convinced Dale Earnhardt Inc. (DEI) management to make some changes for the 2005 season. Eury Jr. switched over to be the crew chief for DEI's second driver, Michael Waltrip. Earnhardt tried several different replacements, but he struggled to establish a good working relationship with all of them.

The 2005 Nextel Cup season turned out to be a disappointing and frustrating one for Earnhardt. He won a race at Chicagoland—a 1.5-mile (2.4km) track where he had not experienced much success before—but otherwise he was not too competitive. Earnhardt finished in the top ten in only thirteen races. He failed to qualify for the Chase for the Cup and ended the year nineteenth in the point standings, a career low. For the third consecutive season, however, Earnhardt received NASCAR's Most Popular Driver Award.

At the end of the 2005 season, DEI restored Eury Jr. as Earnhardt's crew chief. The cousins claimed that their time apart

Tony Eury Jr., left, Earnhardt's cousin and crew chief, left the team for much of the 2005 season after several highly publicized clashes with Earnhardt the year before.

had helped them to repair their relationship and learn to appreciate each other more. Once this change was made, Earnhardt entered the 2006 Nextel Cup season with renewed confidence. He predicted that he would win six or seven races and rank in the top three in the point standings by the start of the Chase. "At this point last year, I really had a question mark of what caliber team I was with," Earnhardt recalled. "I was nowhere near the position I am now as far as how I feel about my team. It's a chemistry we have now with the guys."[66]

The 2006 season started out well for Earnhardt. He won the Crown Royal 400 at Richmond International Raceway in Virginia in May, posting his seventeenth career victory and ending a twenty-seven-race winless streak. But he experienced a series of ups and downs during the remainder of the season. He finished in the top ten in seventeen events, but crashes and engine failures ruined many other outings. Earnhardt still managed to qualify for the Chase, but he ended up finishing fifth in the season standings, 147 points behind Nextel Cup champion Jimmie Johnson. Earnhardt's roller-coaster season did not diminish his standing with fans, though. He was voted NASCAR's most popular driver for the fourth consecutive year.

Chapter 6

Turning in a New Direction

Dale Earnhardt Jr.'s fifth-place finish in the 2006 Nextel Cup point standings was a big improvement over his career-worst nineteenth-place finish the previous year. But NASCAR's most popular driver was not satisfied with fifth place. He only won one race during the 2006 season, after all, and he did not come close to achieving his goal of winning a championship. Earnhardt started to wonder whether he might need to make significant changes in order to compete for a title.

Earnhardt's contract with Dale Earnhardt Inc. (DEI)—the race team founded by his father and owned by his stepmother, Teresa—was due to expire at the end of the 2007 Nextel Cup season. As the two sides began to negotiate the terms of a new contract, it became clear that they held very different opinions about the source of the race team's problems. Teresa Earnhardt blamed Junior for his lack of success. She claimed that his popularity with fans, and his many outside interests, distracted him from the business of racing. In December 2006, Teresa Earnhardt publicly questioned her stepson's commitment in a controversial interview with the *Wall Street Journal*. "Right now the ball's in his court to decide on whether he wants to be a NASCAR driver or whether he wants to be a public personality,"[67] she declared.

Earnhardt, on the other hand, blamed DEI management for his failure to win consistently. He felt that Teresa and others at the company were not willing to commit the resources needed to build a top-notch race team. Junior's uncle, Tony Eury Sr.—who had worked for DEI since Dale Earnhardt Sr. founded the company—agreed with his nephew's assessment of the situation. "There's not a lot of racers running DEI now," said Eury Sr. "There's a lot of money coming in that doesn't get spent in the right places on competition."[68]

Earnhardt wanted to remain with his father's company, but he also longed to compete for championships. Since he did not feel confident that DEI could build elite equipment under current management, he proposed taking on a bigger role in running the race team. He asked his stepmother to let him buy a majority ownership interest in the company, but she refused. As the contract negotiations went on, Earnhardt expressed his frustration toward his stepmother in the media. "Me and Teresa do not see eye to eye. I wish we did, but we don't," he stated. "Man, I look at the fun that other drivers have with their owners. I want a guy who's going to be at the track and give me feedback. I want to feel really part of an entire organization."[69]

Faces Rumors and Speculation

The ongoing negotiations between Earnhardt and DEI was a hot topic as the 2007 NASCAR racing season got underway. At first, most analysts and fans thought that the two sides would eventually reach an agreement. It was common knowledge that Junior and his stepmother did not get along, but most people believed they would conclude that it was in everyone's best interest for Earnhardt to remain part of his father's company.

In April, however, an incident occurred that launched a flurry of rumors and speculation about Earnhardt's future. He was knocked out early during a race at Texas Motor Speedway. As the race continued, the number 5 car driven by Kyle Busch and owned by Hendrick Motorsports was involved in a crash. Thinking that the car was damaged beyond repair, Busch left the track. His pit crew managed to put the car back together before the race ended, but they did not have anyone to drive it. Then

Earnhardt's sometimes rocky relationship with his step-mother Teresa, right, owner of DEI, publicly deteriorated in the mid 2000s, leading to his decision to leave the team that bore his father's name in 2007.

one of the crew members spotted Earnhardt in the garage area, still wearing his driver's suit, and invited him to take a few laps in the repaired machine. Earnhardt jumped at the opportunity to try out the number 5 car, even though he earned points for Busch by doing so.

Afterward, Earnhardt fielded many questions from reporters about his decision to drive a competitor's car. He insisted that he was merely doing a favor for a friend, rather than auditioning for Hendrick or trying to improve his negotiating position with DEI. Still, the incident made many NASCAR insiders wonder if Earnhardt might actually consider moving to a new race team. "The decision by NASCAR's most popular driver to climb into a competitor's car at Texas Motor Speedway certainly stoked the flames of a story line that might have seemed unthinkable before

Teresa Earnhardt publicly questioned her stepson's commitment five months ago," wrote one racing analyst. "Was Earnhardt, as he claimed, merely helping a buddy on Busch's crew and relishing a chance to play the role of the old-school ride-hoppers celebrated on his *Back in the Day* [cable TV] program? Or was the son of a shrewd seven-time champion flexing his business savvy by delivering a veiled threat that no one—not even the team carrying his family name—owns him?"[70]

Leaves the Family Business

Just a month later, Earnhardt delivered the news that had once seemed unthinkable. On May 9, he announced that he was leaving DEI at the end of the 2007 season. He explained that he based the decision on his desire to win a Nextel Cup championship, which he had come to believe was impossible with DEI. "I have no idea how this whole thing is going to play out," he said. "But I do know I had to leave and get out and do my own thing. It's time for me to take charge of my career. It's time for me to start winning championships."[71]

Earnhardt admitted that his poor relationship with his stepmother was a factor in his decision. "Mine and Teresa's relationship has always been very black and white, very strict and in your face," he noted. "It ain't a bed of roses."[72] At the same time, though, he claimed that he had no hard feelings toward DEI and wanted the company to succeed. "If DEI blew up like an atom bomb tomorrow, that'd suck for me even though I'm not there," he said. "I'd be pretty sad. It's important that they still have success, and it's in good shape now."[73]

In some ways, Earnhardt felt that DEI might have a better chance to succeed without him as its lead driver. He argued that the company could make changes and adopt new technology more easily if it was not under constant media scrutiny. "Me getting out of there gives them the opportunity to relax and not be under such a microscope," he stated. "When I was there, you're scared to try new things because the penalty was so large for failure."[74]

Bonding with the New Team Owner

When Dale Earnhardt Jr. decided to switch race teams prior to the 2008 Sprint Cup season, he hoped to join a race team that had an owner with whom he could develop a deep and meaningful connection. He certainly achieved this goal with Rick Hendrick of Hendrick Motorsports.

Hendrick was both a friend and competitor of Dale Earnhardt Sr. and the two men had a great deal of respect for one another. Hendrick first met the younger Earnhardt at a racetrack in 1991. He jokingly asked the sixteen-year-old if he wanted to drive for Hendrick Motorsports someday. When Junior nodded his head excitedly, Hendrick drew up a mock contract on a napkin. "When I mentioned it to Dale [Sr.], he just gave me that look of his," Hendrick remembered. "He knew his son was going to drive for him, not me."

After Dale Jr. got involved in racing, he became close friends with Hendrick's only son, Ricky. They often joked that Dale Jr. would join Hendrick Motorsports when Ricky eventually took over his father's race team. Sadly, Ricky Hendrick was killed in 2004 when a team plane crashed on the way to Martinsville, Virginia.

Both Dale Earnhardt Jr. and Rick Hendrick feel that the tragic deaths of their loved ones created a bond between them. "We have some things in common, unfortunate things," Earnhardt explained. "People will say that Rick will take the place of my daddy or I will take the place of Ricky, but it's not really that. What's happening is that we both understand what the other one has lost. Without using words we know that we've each dealt with some terrible things. And this has built up an incredible trust between us."

Lars Anderson, "Fired Up," *Sports Illustrated*, February 18, 2008, p. 72.

Chooses a New Team

Once Earnhardt announced his departure from DEI, the rumors and speculation centered around where he would land. As the most marketable athlete in the sport, there was no doubt that all of the major race teams would be happy to hire him. So the question became which team made Earnhardt feel most comfortable and gave him the best chance to compete for a title.

Earnhardt sent his cousin and crew chief, Tony Eury Jr. on a mission to visit the shops of several big race teams. Eury Jr. checked out the operations of Richard Childress Racing—which had once boasted Dale Earnhardt Sr. among its drivers—and Joe Gibbs Racing. But Eury Jr. was most impressed with the facilities and atmosphere at Hendrick Motorsports. Known for its engineering expertise and state-of-the-art technology, Hendrick was the most successful team in NASCAR. Earnhardt had family ties to the company, too: his maternal grandfather, car builder Robert Gee, had been one of its original employees.

On June 13, Earnhardt ended the speculation by announcing that he had signed a five-year contract to drive for Hendrick Motorsports, starting with the 2008 Sprint Cup season. He explained that Hendrick had the technology and resources to make him a consistent winner. He also said he felt very comfortable with team owner Rick Hendrick, who was known for

Team owner Rick Hendrick, left, appears with Earnhardt at a news conference in June 2007 to announce the driver's decision to join Hendrick Motorsports in 2008.

developing close, supportive relationships with his drivers. "This is a new day and a new era for me. I can't believe how excited I am," he stated. "And I'll tell you something: it all starts with Rick."[75]

Rick Hendrick was delighted to welcome Earnhardt to his race team, replacing Kyle Busch. But he also acknowledged that taking charge of the career of NASCAR's most popular driver placed him and his operation under a new level of scrutiny. "I can't tell you how thrilled I am and how much pressure I feel," Hendrick noted. "He's such an icon. There's pressure because I want to deliver and there's going to be a lot of people watching."[76]

Earnhardt knew that joining the powerful Hendrick team meant that he would face more pressure as a driver, as well. After all, once he started driving Hendrick's high-performance machines, he could no longer blame his failure to win a championship on poor equipment. Nevertheless, Earnhardt claimed that he looked forward to the challenge. "I understand that I'll have no more excuses starting next year because I'll have as good equipment as anyone," he stated. "Does this make me nervous? Hell, no. I'm a racer, and I just want to win races and contend for championships. Now that I'm with Rick, that's going to start happening. I know it will. What's there to be nervous about?"[77]

Changes Number and Sponsor

Even after Earnhardt announced that he would join Hendrick Motorsports in 2008, he continued to rock the world of NASCAR with news about his future plans. In July 2007 he announced that he was parting ways with Budweiser, his longtime sponsor, due to contract issues with other Hendrick sponsors. Earnhardt had represented Budweiser for most of his racing career. Millions of NASCAR fans associated him with the red number 8 Bud machine and had trouble picturing him in a different car. On the plus side, some marketing analysts predicted that moving away from the beer company sponsorship might expand Earnhardt's appeal to fans younger than the legal drinking age of twenty-one.

On the eve of the 2008 NASCAR season, shoppers in Daytona Beach, Florida, check out merchandise featuring the new number, colors, and sponsor logos adopted by Earnhardt after his move to Hendrick Motorsports.

NASCAR fans received another shock a month later, when Earnhardt announced that he would not be able to take the number 8 with him to his new team. The number, which had once belonged to his grandfather, Ralph Earnhardt, was the property of DEI. Earnhardt tried to arrange a deal that would allow him to continue using it, but the negotiations broke down. He explained that he and his stepmother could not reach agreement over the issues of licensing revenue and ownership of the number after he retired from racing.

In September Earnhardt revealed his new number, paint scheme, and primary sponsors. He announced that his new car number would be 88, another number that his grandfather had once used. His new paint job was green, white, and blue. His two primary sponsors were Mountain Dew/AMP Energy Drink and the U.S. National Guard. One of the only things that stayed the same when Earnhardt moved to Hendrick was that he continued driving a Chevrolet.

All of these changes came as a big shock to NASCAR fans, who pride themselves on showing support for their favorite driver by purchasing clothing and other merchandise bearing his car number and the logos of his major sponsors. "It's one of the biggest sports marketing changes we've ever seen, if not the biggest, because it's happening in a sport where endorsements and sponsorships are more critical than any other sport,"[78] said David Carter, director of the Sports Business Institute at the University of Southern California. Many of Earnhardt's fans seemed willing to stick with him, though, even if it required them to make a complete change in wardrobe. Sales of his merchandise on NASCAR.com increased by 84 percent in the month after he announced the new number and sponsors.[79]

Finishes the 2007 Season

In the meantime, Earnhardt continued driving the red Bud number 8 car for DEI for the remainder of 2007. It turned out to be another disappointing season for him. He experienced a series of mechanical problems that hurt his results. In fact, he went a full season without a victory for the first time in his career. He also led the series with six engine failures and failed to finish a career-high nine races. Earnhardt's best race came in August in Pocono, Pennsylvania, where he qualified on the pole (posted the fastest qualifying time to earn the right to start the race in first place) and finished second to Kurt Busch. He ended the year with seven finishes in the top five and twelve finishes in the top ten. His results were not good enough to qualify for the Chase, and he completed his final season with DEI ranked sixteenth in the point standings.

The frustrations and disappointments of the 2007 season confirmed Earnhardt's decision to join Hendrick Motorsports. Still, he characterized his departure from DEI as a simple difference of opinion about the future direction of the business. He insisted that he felt no bitterness or hard feelings toward DEI or his stepmother. "She's a smart businesswoman,"[80] he noted. "They've beaten Teresa up pretty bad on the Internet, and I don't think that's fair. She's not evil. We just don't get along."[81]

As the 2007 season concluded, Tony Eury Jr. announced that he was leaving DEI to become Earnhardt's crew chief at Hendrick Motorsports. Tony Eury Sr. also left DEI to become operations manager for Earnhardt's race team, JR Motorsports. After moving up to the Busch Series in 2006, Earnhardt purchased a new, 66,000-square-foot shop (6,132sq. m) to develop and build race cars for JR Motorsports.

Teams Up with the Enemy

The full reality of all the changes hit Earnhardt's fans as the start of the 2008 Sprint Cup season approached. They had to face the fact that the next time they saw their favorite driver in action, he would be racing a new car for a different team. To make matters worse, Hendrick Motorsports was not just any team. Partly because it was the most dominant team in NASCAR, it was the one that Earnhardt's fans had always loved to hate. "For Earnhardt Nation, rooting for Hendrick is akin to being a Boston Red Sox devotee cheering for the New York Yankees,"[82] wrote one analyst. Since Earnhardt's fans were used to rooting against Hendrick and

Team owner Rick Hendrick, center, joins his Hendrick Motorsports team—from left, Casey Mears, Jimmie Johnson, Jeff Gordon and Earnhardt—during a NASCAR media event in January 2008.

its very successful drivers, the new season promised to test the strength of fan allegiances.

Many people wondered whether Earnhardt's casual, T-shirt and jeans style would be a good fit with the professional, white-collar image of Hendrick Motorsports. They also questioned whether Tony Eury Jr.—who was known as an old-school mechanic who disliked high-tech gadgetry—would be able to adapt to the way things were done in the Hendrick shop.

Another question in the minds of Earnhardt's fans was how their driver would get along with his new teammates. Hendrick's stable of drivers included four-time Winston Cup champion Jeff Gordon and two-time Nextel Cup champion Jimmie Johnson. Both ranked among the top five NASCAR drivers in popularity and merchandise sales, and combined they won an amazing sixteen races during the 2007 season.

Like most drivers on NASCAR's most competitive circuit, Earnhardt and his new teammates had been involved in a few disputes over the years. After one incident on the track, for instance, Earnhardt called Johnson an idiot. On another occasion, the straight-talking Earnhardt ridiculed Gordon for acting nervous behind the wheel of a car that his mother could drive. "There ain't no hiding the fact that there's competition between me and Jeff," he noted. "Me and Jeff want to beat the hell out of each other."[83]

Among Earnhardt's fans, Gordon was widely considered to be public enemy number one. The California native had won three of his four career titles while competing against Dale Earnhardt Sr. Many people blamed Gordon for Dale Sr.'s failure to win a record-breaking eighth career championship. They also disliked Gordon because his soft-spoken personality and clean-cut image was so different from that of old-time NASCAR drivers. As the 2008 season approached, many Earnhardt fans felt conflicted about him teaming up with his biggest rival. One writer noted that Earnhardt Nation was "salivating at the prospect of its guy in top-notch cars but cringing at the thought of having Gordon as a teammate."[84]

Builds Team Chemistry

Despite the rivalry between Earnhardt and Gordon, team owner Rick Hendrick felt confident that his new driver would fit in. Even though all of the drivers had different personalities and interests, Hendrick predicted that they would develop a strong working relationship. "Our standards are high, and we think 2008 could be a special year for us," he stated. "I can promise you this: All of our guys are going to work together, and we're going to continue to share information between the teams. That's been our formula, and all of our drivers understand that. That issue is not even on my radar."[85]

As soon as Earnhardt officially joined the team, he impressed everyone at Hendrick Motorsports with his focus and determination. He went out of his way to demonstrate his respect for his

Jeff Gordon

Four-time Winston Cup champion Jeff Gordon is one of NASCAR's most popular and successful drivers. The soft-spoken, well-dressed, young hot shot from California first emerged as a rival to Dale Earnhardt Sr. in the mid-1990s. Many fans of The Intimidator felt outraged when Gordon prevented the tough, gruff veteran from claiming a record eighth Winston Cup title. A similar clash in image, driving style, and fan base later developed between Gordon and Dale Earnhardt Jr. When the two drivers became teammates at the beginning of the 2008 season, it turned NASCAR Nation upside down.

Gordon was born on August 4, 1971, in Vallejo, California. Obsessed with racing from an early age, he started out driving tiny quarter-midget cars and won a national championship at age eight. Upon moving up to bigger and faster go-karts, he regularly beat kids twice his age. Gordon moved to Indiana in 1986 and won three sprint car races before he was legally allowed to drive.

In 1991, at the age of nineteen, Gordon won rookie of the year honors in NASCAR's Busch Grand National Series. His performance caught the attention of race-team owner Rick Hendrick, who signed him up to race full time in the Winston Cup series in 1993. Gordon posted seven top-five finishes that year to earn the Raybestos Rookie of the Year Award. Gordon won his first Winston Cup race in 1994, the year Earnhardt Sr. claimed his record-tying seventh career points title.

During the 1995 season, Gordon won seven races and edged out Earnhardt Sr. for the Winston Cup championship. Although Gordon won ten races the following year, he finished second in the point standings to his Hendrick Motorsports teammate Terry Labonte. Gordon came back to win the season-opening Daytona 500 and claim a second Winston Cup championship in 1997. He earned his third title in 1998—the year Dale Jr. made his debut on the Winston Cup circuit—and his fourth in 2001—the year Dale Sr. was killed at Daytona.

The rivalry between four-time Winston Cup winner Jeff Gordon and the Earnhardts has led to countless debates among their fiercely loyal fans.

fellow drivers and his commitment to being a team player. In January 2008, for instance, he flew to Florida to show support for Gordon and Johnson on the first day of on-track testing for the Daytona 500. He spent most of a day hanging around the Hendrick garage and chatting with the drivers and crew members. Gordon felt gratified by his presence, especially since Earnhardt was not scheduled to start his own test sessions until a week later. "Most drivers, if they're not here testing, they don't want to be here," said Gordon. "I think it says a lot. And it's smart, you know, on his part. I'm really proud of him for doing that."[86]

Johnson was equally impressed by Earnhardt's show of interest and support. "It's a credit to his commitment, wanting to be here," he stated. "For him to come down, show the team how committed he is to being up front, winning races and championships, says a lot to his teammates and the racing public."[87] Hendrick was very pleased with the chemistry that developed between his drivers. "When [Earnhardt] went down to Daytona to be with them, they just opened their arms, and it's been almost a lovefest since then,"[88] he related.

Starts Out Strong in 2008

Earnhardt started out strong in his first season driving for Hendrick in 2008. He offered a hint at his potential by winning the Budweiser Shootout, a nonpoints exhibition race held the week of the Daytona 500. Earnhardt looked dominant in his new car, leading forty-seven out of seventy laps. He faced a challenge from Tony Stewart toward the end of the race, but he held on with drafting help from his new teammate, Jimmie Johnson. "This is great for us—exactly what we needed coming out of the gate,"[89] Earnhardt said afterward.

Earnhardt celebrates his win in the Budweiser Shootout at Daytona International Speedway in February 2008, his first event driving for the Hendrick Motorsports team.

Earnhart's success continued a few days later, when he won the Gatorade Duel qualifying race. Although he only managed a ninth-place finish in the season-opening Daytona 500, he showed great consistency over the next few weeks. He finished second in Las Vegas, Nevada; third in Atlanta, Georgia; and fifth in Bristol, Tennessee, giving him four top-ten finishes in the first five races of the year. His strong performances vaulted him to fifth place in the Sprint Cup standings.

As the season went on, though, Earnhardt grew increasingly frustrated by his lack of victories. He came agonizingly close several times over the first fourteen races, but he never quite managed to reach Victory Lane. Earnhardt finally broke through to win his first race for Hendrick Motorsports at the LifeLock 400 at Michigan International Speedway on June 15. He was so low on fuel toward the end that he turned off his engine and coasted along behind the pace car during a caution lap. When the green flag came out with two laps to go, he barely managed to coax the car across the finish line for the eighteenth victory of his career. Earnhardt's fans were thrilled with the dramatic win, which ended his seventy-six-race winless streak in Sprint Cup competition. The victory was made even more meaningful for Earnhardt because it came on Father's Day. "It's special—my daddy meant a lot to me," he stated. "I know I can't tell my father 'Happy Father's Day,' but I get to wish all fathers a happy day. I mean it."[90]

Plans for the Future

Earnhardt felt very pleased with his results in the early part of the 2008 season. He also expressed confidence that his fast start with Hendrick was a sign of great things to come. "These are the best cars. I'm real confident," he declared. "I don't think I have to prove I'm a good race car driver. . . . I want to prove I'm a great one."[91]

In order to join the ranks of the great NASCAR racers—and live up to his father's legacy—Earnhardt knew that he needed to win a championship. The Sprint Cup title was the only thing missing from his list of career accomplishments. By the end of the 2007 season, that list included seventeen race victories, five consecutive Most Popular Driver Awards, and $42 million in prize money—surpassing his father's total career earnings. Earnhardt also earned more than $25 million in endorsements in 2007, making him one of the highest-paid athletes in the world.

Despite his tremendous wealth and fame, however, Earnhardt continues to enjoy life's simple pleasures. He likes nothing more than to escape the spotlight and hang out at home. He shares his property in Mooresville, North Carolina, with an assortment of animals, including two dogs named Killer and Stroker, two cats named Buddy and Tux, and a pair of bison named Laverne and Shirley. His hobbies include playing video games, rebuilding computers, and collecting movie posters. "There's certain things I've been able to do and afford because of racing and winning money," he acknowledged. "But when it really comes down to what gets you by, it's pretty typical stuff. I think that's what really endears [me to] my fans. It's that I'm average."[92]

Introduction: Living Up to the Family Name

1. Quoted in Lee Spencer, "The Ties That Drive," *Sporting News*, August 6, 2001, p. 48.
2. Nate Ryan, "For NASCAR's Top Draw, a More Mature Image," *USA Today*, February 8, 2008, p. A1.
3. Quoted in Gary Graves, "Earnhardt Steadily Shifting Gears," *USA Today*, January 16, 2008, p. C6.
4. Quoted in Lars Anderson, "Fired Up," *Sports Illustrated*, February 18, 2008, p. 72.

Chapter 1: Son of a Racing Family

5. Quoted in Lars Anderson, "Shootin' the Breeze with Junior," *Sports Illustrated*, February 19, 2007, p. 89.
6. Quoted in "Dale Earnhardt," *Biography Today*, April 2001, p. 85.
7. Quoted in Anderson, "Shootin' the Breeze with Junior," p. 89.
8. Quoted in Bob Myers, "Dale Earnhardt, Jr. Q&A," *Circle Track*, April 27, 1998, p. 12.
9. Quoted in NASCAR.com, "The Earnhardts," NASCAR. com, December 20, 2002, www.nascar.com/2002/kyn/families/02/01/earnhardts.
10. Quoted in Leigh Montville, "SI Flashback: Dale Bonding," CNNSI.com, December 22, 1999, http://sportsillustrated. cnn.com/motorsports/news/2001/02/18/earnhardt_and_son_flashback.
11. Quoted in Leigh Montville, "A Father, a Son, a Team," *Sports Illustrated*, May 26, 2004, p. 72.
12. Quoted in Anderson, "Shootin' the Breeze with Junior," p. 89.
13. Quoted in Montville, "A Father, a Son, a Team," p. 72.
14. Quoted in Montville, "A Father, a Son, a Team," p. 72.

15. Quoted in Montville, "A Father, a Son, a Team," p. 72.
16. Quoted in Montville, "A Father, a Son, a Team," p. 72.
17. Quoted in Montville, "A Father, a Son, a Team," p. 72.

Chapter 2: Making His Own Mark

18. Quoted in Myers, "Dale Earnhardt, Jr. Q&A," p. 12.
19. Quoted in Spencer, "The Ties That Drive," p. 48.
20. Quoted in Spencer, "The Ties That Drive," p. 48.
21. Quoted in Loren Mooney, "The Son also Rises," *Sports Illustrated*, June 1, 1998, p. 98.
22. Quoted in David Poole, "The Son also Rises," *Charlotte Observer*, April 5, 1998, p. C3.
23. Quoted in Myers, "Dale Earnhardt, Jr. Q&A," p. 12.
24. Quoted in NASCAR.com, "The Earnhardts."
25. Quoted in Myers, "Dale Earnhardt, Jr. Q&A," p. 12.
26. Quoted in Lars Anderson, "The Road Ahead," *Sports Illustrated*, February 28, 2001, p. 60.
27. Quoted in Daniel McGinn and Bret Begun, "The Son also Races," *Newsweek*, April 15, 2002, p. 46.
28. Quoted in McGinn and Begun, "The Son also Races," p. 46.
29. Quoted in David Poole, "J. Burton Joins Bonus Babies, Holds on for Victory in 600," *Charlotte Observer*, May 31, 1999, p. C1.
30. Dale Earnhardt, Jr. with Jade Gurss, *Driver #8*. New York: Warner Books, 2002, p. 15.

Chapter 3: Death of a Legend

31. Earnhardt, Jr. with Gurss, *Driver #8*, p. 23.
32. Quoted in Lars Anderson, "Growing Up Junior," *Sports Illustrated*, May 26, 2004, p. 12.
33. Earnhardt, Jr. with Gurss, *Driver #8*, p. 85.
34. Quoted in Spencer, "The Ties That Drive," p. 48.
35. Earnhardt, Jr. with Gurss, *Driver #8*, p. 91.
36. Earnhardt, Jr. with Gurss, *Driver #8*, p. 122.
37. Earnhardt, Jr. with Gurss, *Driver #8*, p. 136.
38. Quoted in Earnhardt, Jr. with Gurss, *Driver #8*, p. 137.
39. Quoted in Montville, "A Father, a Son, a Team," p. 72.

40. Quoted in NASCAR.com, "The Earnhardts."
41. Earnhardt, Jr. with Gurss, *Driver #8*, p. 287.
42. Earnhardt, Jr. with Gurss, *Driver #8*, p. 292.
43. Earnhardt, Jr. with Gurss, *Driver #8*, p. 293.
44. Quoted in Anderson, "The Road Ahead," p. 60.
45. Quoted in Ken Garfield, "Earnhardt, Jr., Reflects on Faith, His Father on 700 Club," *Charlotte Observer*, March 22, 2001, p. C3.
46. Quoted in Anderson, "The Road Ahead," p. 60.
47. Quoted in Spencer, "The Ties That Drive," p. 48.
48. Quoted in David Poole, "Earnhardt Conquers Daytona," *Charlotte Observer*, July 8, 2001, p. C1.

Chapter 4: Triumph at Daytona

49. Quoted in Anderson, "Growing Up Junior," p. 12.
50. Quoted in Anderson, "Growing Up Junior," p. 12.
51. Quoted in David Poole, "One for the Son," *Charlotte Observer*, February 16, 2004, p. C6.
52. Quoted in Greg Roza, *Dale Earnhardt, Jr.: NASCAR Driver*. New York: Rosen, 2007, p. 37.
53. Quoted in David Poole, "Junior's Win Was Storybook Moment," *Charlotte Observer*, July 9, 2001, p. C1.
54. Quoted in David Poole, "Junior Gets Win at Track Where He Lost So Much," *Charlotte Observer*, February 16, 2004, p. C1.
55. Quoted in Lars Anderson, "Here Comes Junior," *Sports Illustrated*, October 11, 2004, p. 64.
56. Quoted in McGinn and Begun, "The Son also Races," p. 46.
57. Quoted in David Poole, "Earnhardt Jr. Sweeps First Cup Win at Bristol," *Charlotte Observer*, August 29, 2004, p. C1.

Chapter 5: The Face of NASCAR

58. Quoted in Lee Spencer, "Wiser Bud," *Sporting News*, February 25, 2005, p. 46.
59. Quoted in Anderson, "Growing Up Junior," p. 12.
60. Quoted in Anderson, "Growing Up Junior," p. 12.
61. Quoted in Anderson, "Growing Up Junior," p. 12.

62. Quoted in Mooney, "The Son also Rises," p. 98.

63. Quoted in Jeff MacGregor, "Dale Earnhardt, Jr., and NASCAR Nation," *Sports Illustrated*, July 1, 2002, p. 60.

64. Quoted in Seth Livingstone, "Hanging Out with Junior," *USA Today*, January 12, 2007, p. A1.

65. Quoted in Nate Ryan, "Juniors Achievement," *USA Today*, May 8, 2006, p. C9.

66. Quoted in Ryan, "Juniors Achievement," p. C9.

Chapter 6: Turning in a New Direction

67. Quoted in David Newton, "Teresa Earnhardt Makes Bold Statement in Paper," ESPN.com, December 15, 2006, http://sports.espn.go.com/rpm/news/story/seriesID=28&id=2698958.

68. Quoted in Nate Ryan, "Rites of Passage for Dale Jr.," *USA Today*, November 7, 2007, p. C3.

69. Quoted in Anderson, "Fired Up," p. 72.

70. Nate Ryan, "Jr. Fuels Speculation After Racing Busch's Chevy," *USA Today*, April 20, 2007, p. C11.

71. Quoted in Lars Anderson, "Time to Win," *Sports Illustrated*, December 5, 2007, p. 64.

72. Quoted in A.J. Perez, "Earnhardt Jr. Speaks of Rift with Stepmom," *USA Today*, January 7, 2007, p. C12.

73. Quoted in Ryan, "Rites of Passage for Dale Jr," p. C3.

74. Quoted in Ryan, "Rites of Passage for Dale Jr," p. C3.

75. Quoted in Anderson, "Fired Up," p. 72.

76. Quoted in Nate Ryan, "Much Rides on Junior's Move," *USA Today*, June 14, 2007, p. C1.

77. Quoted in Anderson, "Time to Win," p. 64.

78. Quoted in Ryan, "For NASCAR's Top Draw," p. A1.

79. Ryan, "For NASCAR's Top Draw," p. A1.

80. Quoted in Bill Hewitt, "The Earnhardt Family Smash-Up," *People Weekly*, May 28, 2007, p. 119.

81. Quoted in Ryan, "Much Rides on Junior's Move," p. C1.

82. Ryan, "Jr. Fuels Speculation After Racing Busch's Chevy," p. C11.

83. Quoted in Ryan, "Much Rides on Junior's Move," p. C1.

84. Ryan, "Jr. Fuels Speculation After Racing Busch's Chevy," p. C11.
85. Quoted in Anderson, "Time to Win," p. 64.
86. Quoted in Nate Ryan and Seth Livingstone, "Junior Pays Team Surprise Visit," *USA Today*, January 8, 2008, p. C10.
87. Quoted in Ryan and Livingstone, "Junior Pays Team Surprise Visit," p. C10.
88. Quoted in Seth Livingstone, "Earnhardt Deflects Spotlight onto New Mates," *USA Today*, January 24, 2008, p. C1.
89. Quoted in Seth Livingstone, "Dale Jr. 1-for-1 with New Ride," *USA Today*, February 11, 2008, p. C10.
90. Quoted in Mike Brudenell, "Won and Done," *Detroit Free Press*, June 16, 2008, p. B1.
91. Quoted in Ryan, "For NASCAR's Top Draw," p. A1.
92. Quoted in Livingstone, "Hanging Out with Junior," p. A1.

1974

Ralph Dale Earnhardt Jr. is born on October 10 in Kannapolis, North Carolina.

1980

Earnhardt's father, Dale Earnhardt Sr., wins the first of his seven career Winston Cup championships.

1992

Earnhardt graduates from Mooresville High School and, with his half-brother Kerry, begins fixing up an old car to race in NASCAR's Street Stock division.

1996

With some help from his father, Earnhardt moves up to drive in NASCAR's Late Model Stock division.

1998

Earnhardt moves up to compete full time in the Busch Series for his father's race team, Dale Earnhardt Inc. (DEI). He wins a remarkable seven races during his rookie season to claim the first of two consecutive Busch Series championships.

2000

Earnhardt moves up to race full time at NASCAR's highest level, the Winston Cup Series. Driving the red number 8 Budweiser Chevrolet, he claims his first Winston Cup victory on April 2 at Texas Motor Speedway. His successful rookie season helps him grow closer to his father.

2001

On February 18, NASCAR legend Dale Earnhardt Sr. is killed in an accident on the final lap of the Daytona 500. After struggling to cope with the loss, Earnhardt scores an emotional victory on July 7 in the Pepsi 400—the first Winston Cup race to be held at Daytona since his father's death.

2003

Earnhardt finishes a career-high third in the Winston Cup point standings and is named NASCAR's most popular driver for the first time.

2004

On February 15, Earnhardt roars to victory in the Daytona 500. The win, which comes three years after his father's death in the same race, is one of the greatest moments of his career.

2007

On May 9, Earnhardt shocks the NASCAR world by announcing that he will leave DEI at the end of the season. On June 13, he announces that he has signed a five-year contract to drive for rival Hendrick Motorsports.

2008

Earnhardt officially becomes a part of NASCAR's most successful race team, which also includes top drivers Jeff Gordon and Jimmie Johnson. He makes an impressive debut in his new car—the green, white, and blue number 88 Chevrolet sponsored by Mountain Dew/AMP Energy Drink and the U.S. National Guard.

Books

Larry Cothren and the editors of *Stock Car Racing* magazine, *Dale Earnhardt, Jr.: Making a Legend of His Own.* St. Paul, MN: Motorbooks, 2005. An updated version of Cothren's 2003 book *Dale Earnhardt, Jr.: Standing Tall in the Shadow of a Legend,* this book includes articles about Earnhardt's family background and accounts of key races and events in his career.

Dale Earnhardt, Jr., with Jade Gurss, *Driver #8.* New York: Warner Books, 2002. Earnhardt's best-selling memoir about his rookie Winston Cup season ends with the tragic death of his father in the Daytona 500.

Ken Garfield, *Dale Earnhardt, Jr.: Born to Race.* Berkeley Heights, NJ: Enslow, 2005. This juvenile biography follows Earnhardt's career through the 2004 season and also features background information about NASCAR and Dale Earnhardt Sr.

Greg Roza, *Dale Earnhardt, Jr.: NASCAR Driver.* New York: Rosen, 2007. This readable biography focuses on Earnhardt's childhood, early career, and relationship with his father.

Internet Source

NASCAR.com, "The Earnhardts," December 20, 2002, www.nascar.com/2002/kyn/families/02/01/earnhardts. This lengthy article—part of a series about stock-car racing's most famous families—was published shortly after the death of Dale Earnhardt Sr.

Periodicals

Lars Anderson, "Fired Up," *Sports Illustrated,* February 18, 2008. In this preview of the 2008 Sprint Cup season, Earnhardt discusses his decision to move to Hendrick Motorsports, his relationship with team owner Rick Hendrick, and his hopes for the future.

Jeff MacGregor, "Dale Earnhardt Jr. and NASCAR Nation," *Sports Illustrated*, July 1, 2002. This article examines Earnhardt's rise to stardom and his role in expanding the popularity of NASCAR racing.

Leigh Montville, "A Father, a Son, a Team," *Sports Illustrated*, May 26, 2004. This cover story, first published after Earnhardt's rookie season, explores the evolving relationship between him and his famous father.

Lee Spencer, "The Ties That Drive," *Sporting News*, August 6, 2001. This lengthy article covers Earnhardt's family background and describes his struggles to cope with his father's death.

Web Sites

Dale Earnhardt Jr. (www.dalejr.com). Earnhardt's official Web site includes a brief biography, photos, news articles, race and appearance schedules, and information about his race team, JR Motorsports.

Hendrick Motorsports (www.hendrickmotorsports.com). The official site of Earnhardt's team features news releases, race results, and team biographies.

Merchandise sales, 11, 59, 77
Michigan International
  Speedway, 30–32, 85
Military school, 17
Mitchell Community College,
  20
Most Popular Driver Award, 51,
  57, 67, 68, 86

N
NASCAR
  Back in the Day (television
    show), 63
  Busch Grand National Series,
    25, 25–30
  Chase for the Cup, 52, 54
  comeback season (2001),
    45–47, *46*
  Daytona 500 (2001), 39, *40,
    41*, 42
  Daytona Beach (1955), *16*
  Earnhardt, Ralph, 12–13
  first Winston Cup victory, 33
  history, 15
  Late Model Stock Car division,
    22–24
  point system, 49
  Pontiac Excitement 400, 34,
    36
  popularity, 59, *60–61*, 62
  stock cars, 23, *24*
  Street Stock division races,
    21, 22
  Thunder Special Motegi Coca-
    Cola 500, *31*
  Winston All-Star Exhibition
    Race, *35*
NASCAR seasons
  1998 season, 26–27
  1999 season, 27–28, *28*,
    30–32

2000 season, 33–39
2001 season, 39, *40–41*, 42,
  45–47, *46*
2002 season, 49–51
2003 season, *50*, 51
2004 season, 51–57, *52*, 66
2005 season, 66–67
2006 season, 68, 69
2007 season, 70–71, 78–79
2008 season, 84–85
Nemechek, Joe, 27
Nextel Cup
  2004 season, 51–57, 66
  2005 season, 67–68
  2006 season, 68, 69
  2007 season, 70–71, 78–79
Number 8, 27, 33, 36, 75, 78

O
Obscene language rule violation,
  57

P
Pearson, Larry, 28
Pepsi 400, 45, *46*, 47
Petty, Richard, 58
Pocono 500, *64*
Point system, 49, 53
Pontiac Excitement 400,
  34, 36
Popularity and fame, 29–30,
  58–59, 62–66
Popularity of NASCAR, *60–61*
Private life, 65, 66, 86
Prize money, 18, 57, 86

R
Resentment of other drivers,
  23–24
Rookie year, Winston Cup,
  33–39

Laurie Collier Hillstrom is a partner in Northern Lights Writers Group, a freelance writing and editorial services firm based in Brighton, Michigan. She has written and edited award-winning reference works on a wide range of subjects, including American history, biography, popular culture, and international environmental issues. Recent works include *Defining Moments: Roe v. Wade* (Omnigraphics, 2008), *Frida Kahlo: Mexican Portrait Artist* (Lucent Books, 2007), *The Thanksgiving Book* (Omnigraphics, 2007), and *Television in American Society Reference Library* (UXL, 2006).